Ronan Bennett was brought up in Belfast. He now lives in London. He is the author of two novels, both published by Penguin: *The Second Prison*, which was shortlisted for the *Irish Times*/Aer Lingus First Fiction Award and the David Higham Award, and *Overthrown by Strangers*. He co-wrote *Stolen Years: Before and After Guildford*, Paul Hill's highly praised account of his trial and imprisonment in the aftermath of the Guildford bombings. He has written reviews, articles and essays for the *Guardian*, the *London Review of Books*, *The Times Literary Supplement*, the *Independent* magazine and *Time Out*, and several scripts for television, including the screenplay of a film for the BBC, *Love Lies Bleeding*.

DOUBLE JEOPARDY

THE RETRIAL OF THE GUILDFORD FOUR

FIRST PUBLISHED IN THE *LONDON REVIEW OF BOOKS*

———————

RONAN BENNETT

PENGUIN BOOKS

PENGUIN BOOKS

Published by the Penguin Group
Penguin Books Ltd, 27 Wrights Lane, London w8 5tz, England
Penguin Books USA Inc., 375 Hudson Street, New York, New York 10014, USA
Penguin Books Australia Ltd, Ringwood, Victoria, Australia
Penguin Books Canada Ltd, 10 Alcorn Avenue, Toronto, Ontario, Canada m4v 3b2
Penguin Books (NZ) Ltd, 182–190 Wairau Road, Auckland 10, New Zealand

Penguin Books Ltd, Registered Offices: Harmondsworth, Middlesex, England

First published in the *London Review of Books*, June 1993
Published in Penguin Books 1993
3 5 7 9 10 8 6 4 2

Typeset by Datix International Limited, Bungay, Suffolk
Printed in England by Clays Ltd, St Ives plc
Filmset in Monophoto Baskerville

To Sister Sarah Clarke

ACKNOWLEDGEMENT

I would like to thank Rachel Borrill and Satish Sekar for
help with notes and information

In October 1989 I was in Cuenca in southern Ecuador. Cuenca is a sleepy town, Ecuador – for reasons partly to do with climate and partly with the military's intermittent but pointed interventions in political and economic life – a sleepy country. Once, during a presidential election, the country briefly came out of its quiescence when one of the candidates exhibited worrying signs of sunstroke. In an interview he began to boast about his many personal achievements; by the time he got properly into his stride he was insisting he had a better degree than his opponent, a bigger house, a more beautiful wife, taller children and – definitive proof of his fitness to govern – thicker semen. This was too much, even for Ecuadorians long used to the macho exaggerations of the Latin American stump. The electorate woke up, laughed themselves silly for a week and voted in the candidate of the inferior semen. But this was a rare high point: as a rule, it is a quiet country, a fact reflected in the headline of a newspaper I picked up in Cuenca. For reasons best known to himself, the editor had decided to splash with a story headlined, 'Nothing Unusual Happened Today'. I remember enjoying the story, though I cannot now recall any of the detail. However, another item caught my attention and has stayed with me since: an agency story date-lined Londres to the effect that the Court of Appeal had suddenly and unexpectedly freed the three men and one woman known in Britain as the Guildford Four.

My first reaction was disbelief; later, the news confirmed and the cuttings from London in my hands, I spent a long time pondering the implications. For almost fifteen years Paul Hill, Gerry Conlon, Paddy Armstrong and Carole Richardson had insisted they were innocent and had been framed by the police. I recalled that Sir Michael Havers, who led for the Crown in the 1975 trial, had reasoned to the jury that if the

Four were innocent, a huge conspiracy to pervert the course of justice must have taken place. Where did this leave Havers's conspiracy? Had the Court of Appeal accepted that such a conspiracy had occurred? What did this all mean – not just for the Guildford Four, but for the closely related cases of the Maguire family, the Birmingham Six, Judith Ward? What did it mean for the system of justice in England? Some years earlier, in a judgment in the Birmingham Six case, Lord Denning, the Master of the Rolls, had summed up the broader significance of such a reversal.

> If the six men win. it will mean that the police were guilty of perjury, that they were guilty of violence and threats, that the confessions were involuntary and were improperly admitted in evidence and that the convictions were erroneous. That would mean the Home Secretary would either have to recommend they be pardoned or he would have to remit the case to the Court of Appeal. This is such an appalling vista that every sensible person in the land would say: it cannot be right that these actions should go any further.

With the release of the Guildford Four, Denning's 'appalling vista' had opened up: where was it going to take us?

A distance of four thousand miles and an absence from home of several months can do funny things to one's sense of perspective. Reading the cuts in a provincial town in a small Latin American country. it was easy to get carried away. It seemed to me then that the impossible had happened and that the unimaginable was about to happen; and all in an 'Irish' case, one in which the issues at stake are not just to do with justice, but with politics and polity. I do not think I was being excessively naïve, and certainly wasn't alone. The tenor of the press coverage was one of outrage and anger. When a leader in the *Daily Express* states that 'the process of establishing their innocence took far too long. And those responsible for robbing them of 14 years must be punished', one can be forgiven for thinking that some fundamental shift in perceptions must be underway. Other commentators were even more outspoken. Peter Jenkins in the *Independent* described the law as 'an enemy of justice'. He went on:

> Plainly, after what has happened, radical changes are required in the whole system of police interrogation and in the law relating to confessions. But not only that, the shocking history of the Guildford Four shows that justice must not be left to old men in wigs sitting in judgment over themselves. The authority of the Court of Appeal is in ruins.

In the same reports I read the admissions of Roy Amlot, who appeared for the Crown in the appeal. Material discovered in police files, Amlot told the court, threw 'such a doubt now upon the honesty and integrity' of the investigating officers that 'it would not be right for the Crown to contend that the conviction of any appellant was either safe or satisfactory.' Lord Lane, the Lord Chief Justice, went further. Delivering the court's judgment, he said that 'the officers must have lied', and that 'if they were prepared to tell this sort of lie, then the whole of their evidence becomes suspect.' He continued: 'It is of some comfort to know that these matters are now in the hands of the Director of Public Prosecutions with a view to criminal proceedings being brought. We earnestly express the hope that nothing will be allowed to stand in the way of a speedy progress of those proceedings.' I felt the need to pinch myself. Was this the same Lord Lane I had watched over the course of several weeks in 1987 when he presided over the appeal of the Birmingham Six? Few commended his handling of that case, and no one would say he displayed any obvious sympathy for those before him, or an inclination to believe their allegations of police malpractice. But now Lane, the country's senior judge, was admitting that a gross wrong had been perpetrated; and he was saying that the policemen responsible should be punished.

*

With Denning's appalling vista now wide open, there were
renewed demands for a fresh look at other contentious convictions. The Guildford Four's release was followed by the
Crown's capitulation in the cases of the Maguire family,
the Birmingham Six, Judith Ward, the Tottenham Three
and the Cardiff Three; all had their appeals upheld.

'British justice' resonates powerfully as a shibboleth for those
who like to pride themselves in Britain's supposed traditions of
fairness and impartiality, and the Briton's innate sense of fair
play; it is an ideal intricately bound up with notions of
Britain's status, worth and civilizing mission. In the words
of tabloid leader writer Ronald Spark: 'The British system of
justice is one of the most precious parts of our heritage. From
the time of Magna Carta, we set the pattern that enlightened
countries all over the world would follow.' One might have
expected that the release of so many wrongly imprisoned
men and women would have shamed into silence those fond of
broadcasting the virtues of this 'most precious part of our
heritage'. Not a bit of it. An unblushing few even claimed the
releases demonstrated the system's soundness.

If, for some, Guildford had become emblematic of the corruption and failure at the heart of the system of criminal justice in
this country, for others it represented merely a regrettable
failure of nerve on the part of those who should have known
better, and who should have been able to resist the blandish-
ments of liberal opinion and put a lid on attempts to sully the
name of 'British justice'. No sooner had Lord Lane delivered
his judgment in the case of the Guildford Four than it began
to be whispered in darker corners and cloisters that all was not
as it seemed, that public opinion had been led astray by
irresponsible journalists who had rushed in without being in
full possession of the facts, that some or all of the Four – the
versions varied   were guilty. The 'whispering campaign', as
defenders of the Four described it, mostly took the form of off-
the-record briefings to journalists who. though they were un-

willing or unable to repeat in their copy the substance of what they had heard, showed signs that they were being influenced. Joshua Rozenberg, the BBC's legal affairs correspondent, began to wonder aloud about the significance of the wording of Lord Lane's judgment. When upholding an appeal, Rozenberg said, it was usual for judges to describe convictions as 'unsafe and unsatisfactory'. Lane had said only that the Guildford convictions were 'unsafe'. The absence of the full form, Rozenberg suggested, might be evidence that while the judges were not convinced in law that the convictions could be sustained, they weren't convinced either that the Four were innocent. It seemed to me at the time a very small point on which to base so large a claim, but of such whimsies was the whispering campaign composed.

Senior figures in the judiciary were prepared to say in private that the Four were guilty; journalists relayed unchallenged comment and gossip on a lobby basis. Occasionally the whispers were given full barking voice by the more injudicious of the judiciary. On the occasion of his retirement as Recorder of London in July 1990, Sir James Miskin gave a television interview to the BBC. "That was a mad decision, was it not?' he said of the Court of Appeal's judgment in the Guildford case. 'They didn't give any thought to the fact that three years after it had happened there was a full appeal and there was no suggestion from any source that police documentation showed that the confessions had been cooked up.' After a newspaper article appeared in which some of the Four said they intended to sue, Miskin contacted their lawyers and retracted his statement. Then Lord Denning spoke up, telling the *Spectator* that it would have been better if the Birmingham Six had been hanged so as to avoid all these damaging campaigns on behalf of plainly guilty men. Like Miskin, Denning apologized after hearing rumours of legal action.

As the debate over Guildford – and, by extension, the cases of the Maguires, the Birmingham Six and Judith Ward –

intensified, so it became more politically and ideologically charged. There is a striking homogeneity about the political outlook and identity of those opposed to the Court of Appeal's verdict: by and large they are the conservative defenders of, and those who have a direct interest in, the institutions of British justice – the judiciary, the police, the political Right. By contrast, supporters of the Guildford Four are a politically heterogeneous bunch: at one end, Cardinal Basil Hume, Robert Kee, Merlyn Rees, Lord Scarman and the late Lord Devlin; at the other, rhetoric-ridden, far-left Trotskyist groupings. And in between, the world and its dog. The only thing on which all are agreed – some with more knowledge of the facts than others – is that Paul Hill, Gerry Conlon, Paddy Armstrong and Carole Richardson were not in any way connected with the bombings.

I must declare an interest. I first heard the name of Paul Hill when I was myself in prison. The year was 1975 and the prison Long Kesh, the encampment of Nissen huts and razor-wire hastily assembled by British squaddies to hold the Republican enemies of British rule in Northern Ireland. I heard Hill's name spoken on the radio the day he was sentenced to life imprisonment for the murder of five people at Guildford and another two at Woolwich. The judge recommended that he be released only in the event of grave illness or extreme old age. Paul Hill, aged 21, had in effect been sentenced to remain in prison until the morning of his death.

Like Hill and his co-accused, I was released from my wrongful imprisonment by the Court of Appeal, mercifully after a much shorter time inside. I write, then, as a former prisoner, and I write as an Irishman, as someone who believes that the ramifications of the Guildford case say as much about Britain's unhappy relationship with Ireland as they do about the system of criminal justice in this country. And I write as someone who, six years ago, became involved in the Guildford case (in a peripheral way) at the request of Hill's family. By then lawyers and journalists had between them uncovered a great deal of new evidence that pointed to the innocence of the Four. The more I read of the documentation, the more I talked to people connected with the case, the more I became convinced the Four were innocent. I was abroad when they were released but returned soon afterwards, and in 1990 I collaborated in writing *Stolen Years*, Hill's account of his trial and imprisonment. In doing so I learned still more about the case, every detail hardening my belief that not only were the Four innocent but that their conviction in 1975 was the result not of error but of deliberate wrongdoing. For all these reasons there is undoubtedly a gap between the way I see the case and what I see in it, and the way the case appears to Miskin, Denning and those who take their view. If this gap is bridgeable it can only be by means of a common interest in the integrity of the law – not the law as the shrine before which the epigones of Hale and Blackstone worship, but the law as a set of rational and known rules, agreed rather than imposed, and applicable to all in equal measure.

To both sides, the release of the Guildford Four was Round One; Round Two was the prosecution of those accused of having framed them. For defenders of the Four the prosecution would be the acid test of whether British justice could face up to what had been done in its name. For opponents, the prosecution was unnecessary, a further pointless exercise in undermining the reputation of the legal system and the morale of the police.

The evidence for the prosecution had been uncovered by a team of Avon and Somerset detectives originally formed in August 1987 after Douglas Hurd, then Home Secretary, asked Jim Sharples, then Deputy Chief Constable of the Avon and Somerset Force, to investigate new alibi evidence submitted on behalf of Paul Hill. Two years later, as a result of the inquiry into that evidence, Hurd referred the case to the Court of

Appeal. It was only then that detectives from the Sharples team went to Guildford Police Station to collect all the files. The case already had a cast of thousands who between them had generated an astonishing amount of paperwork. The Sharples team found fourteen files containing some 29,000 documents, some only a few lines long, others containing many, many pages: handwritten interview notes, typed reports, witness statements, forensic reports, briefs, transcripts, exhibits, internal information documents, minutes of meetings, memos, letters, confidential intelligence reports.

Among the documents, a detective inspector discovered something of interest in Patrick Armstrong's 'personal file': a set of typed notes containing many handwritten amendments. In their amended form, the typed notes were an almost word-for-word match with manuscript notes of three interviews with Armstrong on 4, 5 and 6 December 1974. These rough typed notes, as they became known, aroused the interest of the Sharples team because the officers who had conducted the interviews had always maintained that the manuscript notes had been made contemporaneously, that they had been written down as the questions were put and the answers given. But if the manuscript was a contemporaneous note of the interviews, what were the rough typed notes for? And how was it that the manuscript – which, if the interviewing officers had been telling the truth, must have come first – contained many of the handwritten amendments found on the rough typed notes? Surely, the Sharples team reasoned, it is more usual for the draft document to contain the amendments and deletions: the rough typed notes gave every appearance of being a draft for the supposedly contemporaneous mauscript.

The team immediately appreciated that if this was true – if the rough typed notes were a draft – then the manuscript could not have been recorded contemporaneously. But the three officers connected with these documents – Vernon Attwell, John Donaldson and Thomas Style – had signed witness statements in December 1974 stating that the manuscript notes were contemporaneous, and they had repeated this on oath in the trial in 1975. If the rough typed notes were indeed a draft from which the manuscript notes were later composed, Attwell, Donaldson and Style had seriously misled the court about the nature of the interviews.

In the summer of 1989 the Sharples team invited Attwell, Donaldson and Style to give an explanation of the rough typed notes. Nothing is known of what went on in these interviews, except that the three men were not cautioned. It may be assumed that whatever they said convinced neither the Sharples team nor the DPP that there was an innocent explanation for the rough typed notes because the DPP then requested an immediate hearing before the Court of Appeal. On 19 October, Roy Amlot, counsel for the Crown, announced that his instructions were not to seek to uphold the convictions. Amlot addressed the judges on the discovery of the rough typed notes:

> Amongst the papers that had been kept by the Surrey police, the Avon and Somerset officers discovered the following documents: first, rough draft notes of each of the three interviews with Armstrong over three days. The notes were typewritten with a large number of alterations in manuscript . . . In their altered form they match almost word for word a separate set of manuscript notes of interview used by the officers in the trial. In the trial the officers claimed that the manuscript notes were made during each interview as contemporaneous notes. If that were so, it is difficult to see why the set of draft notes was brought into existence. It is impossible to see why the draft notes take the form they do unless they were made before the manuscript notes. If they were, the manuscript notes cannot have been made during the interviews, nor can the officers offer a satisfactory explanation now. The inescapable conclusion is that no contemporaneous notes were made of each interview, as indeed was suggested by the defence at

the trial, and that the officers seriously misled the court . . . The
Crown says that not only did the officers, all three of them   and
not just junior officers   mislead the court, but that because of the
way the notes had been prepared, and because of the statements
that those officers made in 1974 for the purposes of the trial, it is
clear that they agreed together to present their notes to the court
in this fashion.

Amlot was alleging that the three officers had entered into a
conspiracy to pervert the course of justice. The judges agreed,
condemned the officers in ringing terms and quashed the
convictions of the Four.

Although Lord Lane went on to express the hope that
prosecution would follow speedily, Regina v. Vernon Weir
Attwell, John Sutherland Donaldson and Thomas Lionel Style
was a long time coming. It was not until the summer of 1990,
a year after the discovery of the suspect notes, that the three
detectives were invited to attend a formal interview in London,
accompanied by their solicitors. The three men declined to say
anything, taking advantage of the rule against self-incrimination so often attacked by the police themselves. Another four
months passed before, on 22 November 1990, the Crown
Prosecution Service announced that the three detectives were
to be charged with conspiracy to pervert the course of justice.

Under normal circumstances – more accurately, with
normal, non-police defendants – a trial could be expected
within six to nine months. In June 1991, however, lawyers for
the detectives made an abuse of process application, arguing
that the case be dismissed on the grounds that their clients
could not expect a fair trial after the adverse publicity and
after such a lapse of time; and further protesting that when
originally questioned, in the summer of 1989, by members of
the Sharples team, the three detectives had not been cautioned.
On 11 June 1991 the stipendiary magistrate, Ronald Bartle,
upheld the application and dismissed the case. The following

month, the DPP sought leave for judicial review of Bartle's decision; this the High Court granted in October. In January 1992 the High Court reversed Bartle's decision and the charges were reinstated. In normal circumstances a trial would have taken place soon afterwards. Yet in March 1992 the defence succeeded in having the trial fixed for April 1993 – an extraordinary delay.

One of those who complained about the postponements was Sir John May. Sir John, a retired Court of Appeal judge, had been appointed by the Government to head a judicial inquiry into the Guildford case after the release of the Four (his report is expected later this year). The delays forced Sir John to suspend his public hearings and interrupted other aspects of the inquiry's work. When Sir John complained to Barbara Mills, the DPP, that the case against the three detectives could have been heard 'far more quickly', he received a letter in which he was reminded in curt tones of the case's 'sensitivity'. Sir John was also 'respectfully' requested to correct any impression he may have given that he had been 'criticizing the Director for the delay which had occurred'.

So it was not until 20 April 1993, almost four years after the rough typed notes had first come to light, that Attwell, Donaldson and Style took their place in the dock of Court Eight at the Old Bailey. The length of time it had taken to get the men to trial was interpreted by some as indicating a certain lack of enthusiasm for the task in hand on the part of the Crown. And there were other, graver doubts about the prosecution: first, why was it restricted to Attwell, Donaldson and Style? (The DPP has acknowledged that thirteen of the investigating officers had been under suspicion and examined by the Sharples team.) In the 1989 appeal, Amlot had told the court that the rough typed notes were only one of several sets of suspicious documents:

Other records have revealed disquieting aspects of the case. The
detention sheets for each appellant (which do not appear to have
been either required or made available in the trial) – and they
record the suspect's movements around the police station – reveal
a disturbing difference between the number and times of interviews
according to the sheets, and the number and times of interviews
according to the officers in evidence. Interviews are shown on the
sheets which were never given in evidence or revealed to the
Director of Public Prosecutions or prosecuting counsel. Interviews
are shown on the sheets as taking place at markedly different times
from those given in court by the interviewing officers, and the
discrepancies apply to each appellant.

Amlot cited one example in which the detention sheets showed
up a nine-hour interview with Hill not recorded by the police
or revealed by the relevant officers in court. It had always
been Hill's case that during his interrogation in Guildford
Police Station he had been questioned for lengthy periods, and
that some of these interviews had not shown up in the official
record. The police had always denied this. What the Sharples
team had found was the documentary evidence – including
duplicate detention sheets – to support Hill's version.

Nor did it end there. Amlot went on to tell the appeal
judges:

The Avon and Somerset officers discovered a set of manuscript
notes relating to [another] interview with Hill. The notes have
been identified by one of the officers concerned. The interview as
revealed by the notes was never tendered in evidence and had not
been disclosed to the Director of Public Prosecutions or to prosecuting counsel. It relates to relevant and significant matters. It is
clear from the content of the notes that it took place two days after
Hill had been charged and led to his fifth statement under caution.
It is clear that these officers also seriously misled the court. The
content of the notes bears no resemblance to the evidence given by
the officers as to the way in which they claim Hill 'volunteered' to

> make his fifth statement. The inescapable conclusion is that the
> true interview was suppressed and a false version given by the
> officers in court . . . one is driven to the inescapable conclusion
> that this piece of evidence was concocted.

As with the duplicate detention sheets, and the discrepancies
between them and the evidence given in court, the notes
relating to this interview with Hill did not lead to charges
against any of the officers concerned. The DPP decided privately that there was insufficient evidence to prosecute the
officers who had, in Amlot's words, 'seriously misled the court'.
Nor could this additional evidence be used to further the case
against Attwell, Donaldson and Style, since the DPP had
decided to prosecute the narrower and more specific conspiracy
based solely on the alleged fabrication of Armstrong's interview notes.

And there is more. I have been shown two sets of documents,
not mentioned by Amlot, whose relevance was either not
noticed or not appreciated by the Sharples team. The first is a
photocopy of the original handwritten note of an interview
with a young Irishman named John McGuinness, one of
several friends and acquaintances of Armstrong, Hill, Conlon
and Richardson taken into custody in December 1974. Although he was later cleared of any involvement, at the time of
his detention the police seemed to think McGuinness an important suspect. Present at one interview were a senior officer and
two constables, one of whom recorded the interview contemporaneously – at least that was what the police claimed in their
section nine witness statements. (Sometimes called 'police witness statements', these are typed versions of the manuscript
notes prepared in the police station by civilian typists for use
in later proceedings, and normally relied on – for ease of
reading – in the trial.) The typed police witness statement
relating to the McGuinness interview – a photocopy of which
is the second set of documents I have been shown – was made

on 8 January 1975. It was based on the manuscript note supposedly recorded during the interview. The interview took place in Woking Police Station on 7 December 1974. The first question runs:

> Sit down J weve spoken to Pad & Carol & they have put U right in it. & said U were involved in bombing the 7 Stars PH in gld at 9:30 pm on 5 Oct 75

In the typed police witness statement the 'contemporaneous' manuscript is rendered:

> Sit down John, we've spoken to Paddy and Carol and they have put you right in it and said you were involved in bombing the Seven Stars Public House in Guildford at 9:30 p.m. on the 5th October 1974.

The only discrepancy of any significance is in the date of the bombings. In the typed version it is given correctly: '5th October 1974'. In the manuscript note – which, remember, the three officers claimed was recorded at the time of the interview, on 7 December 1974 – the year of the bombing is wrong: '5 Oct 75'. Someone noticed the mistake and wrote 4 over the 5 of 75. The amendment is significant, for it leads to the question: how did the officer, writing in December 1974, come to write '1975'? We frequently persist in lagging a year behind when dating our letters and cheques in January or February; but we rarely, if ever, leap forward a year when writing at the beginning of December. Is it possible that these three officers – as in the allegation against Attwell, Donaldson and Style – were putting together a manuscript note sometime after the interview, which they then passed off as a contemporaneous record? The confusion over the year suggests that if this was the case, the 'contemporaneous' note may have been written in 1975, possibly around the time the civilian typist was preparing the police witness statements (8 January), but in any case long after the actual interview.

*

What conclusions are we to draw from the existence of so many sets of amended documents? Does it suggest that the practice of doctoring interview notes and their supporting documentation was so common as to be almost routine? Does it point to a wider conspiracy within the Guildford police? Certainly there is enough suspect material – involving a very large proportion of the interviewing officers – to suggest that something very odd was going on, and that it was not just confined to the alleged conspiracy of Attwell, Donaldson and Style. This material implies an exercise of considerable complexity, one requiring a high degree of co-ordination. In which case, should the charge of conspiracy to pervert the course of justice have been restricted to only three officers? Should the whole body of evidence relating to suspicions of wider wrongdoing not have been adduced in a more broadly focused trial? And should the prosecution have been limited to police officers?

In the 1989 appeal, Amlot had been careful to place the blame entirely on the police. More than once he emphasized that officers had withheld significant material from the DPP and prosecuting counsel. Yet it has been fully demonstrated that the DPP and prosecuting counsel themselves withheld significant material from the defence at the time of the trial in 1975 and subsequently. Amlot was silent on this point. In particular, he failed to explain how crucial alibi evidence for Gerry Conlon had not been disclosed to his lawyers before the trial. At the time of the Guildford bombings, Conlon had been staying at a hostel in Kilburn run by the Catholic Church for young Irishmen. In January 1975, after Conlon had been charged, the police arrived at the hostel to question the residents. One, Charles Burke, gave a statement in which he said he had seen Conlon asleep in bed on the night of the bombing. The police passed Burke's statement to the DPP, who subsequently sent it to the prosecution team, led by the late Sir Michael Havers; the juniors were Michael Hill, Paul Purnell and Philip Havers (Sir Michael's son). The three juniors at a later point signed a note listing, among others, Conlon's alibi witnesses. They included Burke's name on the list. However, a separate list later made available to the defence unaccountably omitted any mention of Burke.

Neither the DPP nor any of the prosecution team told Conlon's lawyers of the existence of Burke's statement. Many years later, Gareth Peirce, Conlon's solicitor, discovered in Guildford Police Station an interesting bundle of documents, labelled in typescript: 'Not to be disclosed to the defence'. The bundle included Charles Burke's statement. In the trial Conlon told the jury that he spent the night of the bombing in bed after a heavy afternoon drinking session. He was unable to call Burke – who had since returned to Ireland – because the DPP and the prosecution team had kept Burke's statement to themselves. In his summing-up, Mr Justice Donaldson drew the jury's attention to the fact that although Conlon had claimed to have an alibi, there was no 'independent witness to support him'. Although Michael Hill, Purnell and Havers are said to be 'furious' about any hints of impropriety (Hill, a former chairman of the Criminal Bar Association, is reported as saying the case was conducted 'not just in accordance with the rules, but in the spirit behind the rules'), no explanation has been made public for the astonishing failure of the police, the Crown and the DPP to inform Conlon's legal advisers of their client's alibi.

The matter of Conlon's alibi does not rest there. When the police visited the Kilburn hostel in January 1975, they also removed records relating to the residents, which they refused to return when Peirce was trying to trace those who had been staying in the hostel in October 1974. It was not until 1988, after Father Frank Ryan, the hostel's head, had sued the police, that copies – not the originals – were returned. Peirce was then at last able to start tracing potential witnesses. It emerged that a nun working in the hostel in 1974, Sister Power, had also given a statement to the police about Conlon's movements. This statement was similarly suppressed, and was discovered in the same bundle as Burke's – the bundle marked 'Not to be disclosed to the defence'. What possible reason was there for not disclosing this information? Until the matter is clarified in public, it is difficult to interpret it as anything other than a willingness on the part of some of the police, the DPP and the prosecution team to withhold evidence from the court about Conlon's whereabouts on the night of the bomb-ings. Gareth Peirce is convinced that the DPP's failure to defend the appeal in October 1989 was an attempt by the authorities to avoid having to explain in public the misconduct of the police. Not only that. The brevity of the hearing, she also says, prevented the appellants from bringing out what would seem to be the much larger and still more serious evidence of misconduct by the DPP and prosecuting counsel over non-disclosure. Peirce insists that a full hearing of all the evidence in 1989 would have incontrovertibly demonstrated the innocence of the Guildford Four. At the very least the Crown made sure that the wider body of evidence of malpractice and wrongdoing was not fully aired in open court; and by limiting the prosecution for conspiracy to pervert the course of justice to just three officers, the DPP made sure that the larger body of suspect material never saw the light of day in Court Eight.

Asked how he felt about the three officers, Paddy Armstrong replied simply that he hoped they would get a fair trial. He need not have worried on that score. From the beginning, scrupulous care was paid to their rights and well-being. When, in the summer of 1990, the Sharples team got round to confronting them with the rough typed notes, the three suspects were invited – not brought – to London. The suspects' lawyers were in constant attendance; and when the suspects took full advantage of the right to silence they were not locked up in an effort to encourage them to change their minds, but immedi-ately set free on bail, and not just bail but unconditional bail.

After paying a sum into court (later returned), they were granted legal aid. And when the time at last came for trial, they were not driven at breakneck speed through the streets of London to the Old Bailey in an armoured police van – motor-cycle outriders alongside, helicopters above and police marksmen on the roof of the court   but invited to attend by letter. I would be the last to say this is a bad thing: I would be the first to say that it is far from the norm.

But then these defendants were far from the norm. It is not unknown for policemen and women to land in the dock. But most of those who do are there for reasons of private corruption. There is a distinction in the police force between 'bent for yourself' and 'bent for the job'. The first term speaks for itself; the second has to do with what Paul Condon, the new Metropolitan Commissioner, has called 'noble cause corruption' – the breaking of rules by officers who are acting, not with the motive of gain for themselves, but out of an overdeveloped sense of loyalty to the job. 'Noble cause corruption' occurs when the police have in custody a suspect they are convinced is guilty but lack the evidence to prove it. In such circumstances officers may, in their own words, 'enhance', 'firm up', 'embroider', 'bolster' or 'boost' the evidence, by inventing verbal admissions (what used to be known as 'verbals') or planting incriminating evidence. Policemen who are 'bent for themselves' are a disgrace to the force; those who are accused of being 'bent for the job' deserve sympathy and understanding. So it was that every morning Attwell, Donaldson and Style – three detectives accused of being bent for the job – approached the revolving doors of the Old Bailey as free men. During a break in the judge's summing-up. Attwell's police mates met him at the entrance. It was their normal practice to retire for a drink to a nearby pub. 'Sorry, lads,' Attwell, cigar in hand, told them on this occasion, 'they told me I have to stay within the precincts of the court.' It was the nearest any of the three men came to experiencing a restriction on their personal liberty.

Vernon Weir Attwell is now aged 52. He is a heavy-set man who bears more than a passing resemblance to Jimmy Greaves; and he shares something of the former footballer's manner of speech and gesture. Attwell began his career in the police as a Metropolitan cadet in 1955, joining the force as a constable two years later. He transferred to Surrey in 1962. By the account of Edmund Lawson QC, his counsel, Attwell was a detective of limited ability. During the Guildford investigation, he was the junior officer in the team led by Detective Chief Inspector Thomas Style, for whom he acted as driver, scribe and typist. Attwell, Lawson was to say, was no candidate for Mensa; another defending barrister referred to him as a man who appeared to have difficulty 'with what used to be called joined-up writing'. Those defending Attwell had good reason to play up his supposed deficiencies. Would someone of limited capacity for intelligent thought have been capable of taking part in what would have had to have been a fairly complex operation to frame Paddy Armstrong? As for his supposedly limited writing ability, an important plank in the defence case was the contention that the rough typed notes might have been prepared for ease of reading. But we should be careful not to allow our impression of the man to be too highly coloured by the defence's description: Attwell had managed to get off the beat, out of uniform and into the CID, and by the time he retired he had received a total of nine commendations for persistence and detective work. After almost thirty years in the force, he now works as a security guard in Surrey.

Next on the indictment was John Sutherland Donaldson. Donaldson left the Surrey Force five years ago with the rank of detective sergeant, having joined in 1958. He looks considerably older than his 57 years, and gives the appearance of having a less than driving personality. One of his golfing friends told me he was 'a good bloke, straight, a mild man'. The idea of him doing wrong just didn't gel. 'He wouldn't fart without his wife's permission.' Like Attwell, Donaldson was assigned to Style's team for Armstrong's interrogation in December 1974. He was awarded long service and good conduct medals, but it is said that he believes he was denied a civilian job with the police after being charged in connection with the Guildford case. He is now unemployed.

Thomas Lionel Style, now 59, is said to be suffering from emphysema, which would account for the thinness of the man and his voice. As ironic coincidence would have it, emphysema is the disease that afflicted Gerry Conlon's father Giuseppe, who was sentenced to twelve years on a charge of handling explosives and whose conviction, as part of the scandalous Maguire case, was one of those the Court of Appeal overturned many years later. During the trial in Court Eight, Thomas Style was allowed to leave the dock to use his nebulizer: Giuseppe Conlon was given compassionate parole to leave prison the day after he died. Of the three men on trial, Style had much the most distinguished career, reaching the rank of chief superintendent before his retirement in 1984, after which he went to work for the Ministry of Defence, where, as his barrister coyly put it, 'he was employed in a sensitive position', and 'was promoted and put in charge of a team'. It appears he carried out positive vetting. In the dock, Style, in common with his two co-defendants, gave a rather subdued impression. This was understandable: criminal trials are harrowing, even when one is treated with the courtesy extended to these men. It may be that no amount of consideration would have been enough to ward off the shame of finding themselves where they were: these were, after all, men of 'impeccable reputation', as their lawyers and the judge reminded the jury on several occasions. Such men are unaccustomed to being in the dock; it was uncomfortable for them and it showed.

The trial opened at 10.30 a.m. on 20 April 1993 before Mr Justice Macpherson, a High Court judge and former colonel in the SAS. The clerk of the court read out the charges – that

Attwell, Donaldson and Style had conspired to pervert the course of public justice between 2 December 1974 and 23 October 1975 – to which the defendants pleaded not guilty. Six men and six women then took their place in the jury-box, and Mr Julian Bevan QC stood up to open for the Crown. According to lawyers and journalists who have observed him at work, Bevan is a 'pleasant, mild sort of man', 'jolly in a hail-fellow-well-met sort of way', 'nice, but lacking the instinct for the jugular needed by a prosecutor'. Bevan first outlined the events at Guildford on 5 October 1974 when two bombs exploded, in the Seven Stars and the Horse and Groom public houses, killing five people and injuring seventy, and at Woolwich a month later when a bomb, thrown through a window of the King's Arms, went off and killed two customers.

Bevan then told the jury that Paddy Armstrong had been one of several people detained in November and December 1974 in connection with the bombings. Armstrong was central to this trial because the documents at the heart of the Crown case related to interviews the three men now in the dock had conducted with him over several days of questioning. During his interrogation, Armstrong made statements under caution confessing to both the Guildford and the Woolwich attacks. In the 1975 trial, Bevan went on, Armstrong claimed he had only made the confessions after he 'had been hit, reduced to tears, intimidated, and that most of these admissions were in response to suggestions' from the officers themselves. Bevan said Attwell, Donaldson and Style had persistently denied they had treated Armstrong improperly, and it did not form part of the Crown's case in these proceedings that Armstrong had been abused in any way. As to the charge of conspiracy to pervert the course of justice, the three former detectives, Bevan said, 'refuted the allegations, saying the handwritten notes were contemporaneously written'. However, it was the Crown's case that Attwell, Donaldson and Style had conspired together after interviewing Armstrong to copy out the manuscript notes of the interviews, based on 'rough typed notes' prepared by Attwell and bearing amendments in the handwriting of all three accused. The three officers then passed off the manuscript as a contemporaneous record. "The sad truth is that so-called contemporaneous notes were not contemporaneous at all but had been compiled after the interview. It is the Crown case that these three defendants lied about the origin of these notes in order to bolster their own case.' The jury, Bevan said, would have to decide whether the manuscript notes or the rough typed notes came first: 'My submission is that the typed came first.' If so, the three detectives were guilty of conspiracy to pervert the course of justice. Bevan stated that it was irrelevant to the Crown's case whether Armstrong was innocent or guilty: the jury had to consider only the question of the origin of the two sets of notes. 'Police officers have no licence to lie or to cheat, whatever the case, whatever the crime, and that includes murder,' Bevan said.

He then began to read out extracts from Armstrong's confessions. In addition to involvement in the Guildford and Woolwich bombings, Armstrong had admitted under interrogation to membership of the IRA, taking part in sniper attacks against Protestants in Belfast, shooting at soldiers, and participating in a series of robberies of bookmakers' shops. Armstrong's admissions about the robberies were particularly damaging because the owners, Bevan said, had been too frightened of IRA reprisals to report them to the police. How could Armstrong possibly have known about them if he himself had not participated in them? The jury also heard that Armstrong had provided the police with the names of ten men he claimed were IRA activists, and that Armstrong had repeated the substance of his confessions to RUC officers from Belfast in January 1975, after he had been remanded to prison and when there was no question of oppression. It was, on the face of it, damning stuff. Damning, that is, not to those on trial, but to Armstrong, and it was used throughout the trial by the defence and by the judge as suggestive of Armstrong's guilt.

Bevan could have pointed out – but chose not to – that Armstrong knew of one of the bookie robberies because he was working as a boardmaker in the shop when it was robbed. He was a victim of the robbery, not its perpetrator. No details about the times, dates or scenes of the other alleged robberies were heard in Court Eight and no witnesses called to confirm that they had occurred (in fact, no information about these robberies has ever been disclosed); but, assuming the robberies did take place, it is unlikely that, in a community as small and close-knit as that of West Belfast, such events would not have been widely known and discussed. Similarly, neither the police nor the Crown has ever provided details about the other Belfast incidents in which Armstrong is supposed to have been involved; the only evidence that they even took place is Armstrong's uncorroborated confession. The names of 'IRA activists' which Armstrong gave to the police were those of local men, some of whom were commonly known to have been in the IRA; as for their ranks, he simply made them up.

Perhaps still more damning was Armstrong's failure to appear in court to testify against the three officers. Edmund Lawson QC, for Attwell, took up this theme on the second day of the trial: 'While Armstrong and his advisers might be prepared to make public announcements and submissions to Sir John May in his inquiry, they are not prepared to help us, not prepared to help the prosecution and not prepared to help you.' Armstrong's absence was raised time and again by the defence and by the judge as being strongly suggestive of Armstrong's guilt. Why else was he not in court? The jury was told repeatedly that Armstrong had been invited to appear but 'had refused'. Bevan argued that, because of Armstrong's alleged involvement in the IRA, his value to the jury would have been 'less than zero'. The defence did not think so. Lawson told the jury: 'If I'd had that man in the box to cross-examine, then we would have seen the truth.' Armstrong's absence was undoubtedly a telling point against the Crown.

'Considerable efforts,' Bevan said, 'were made on the part of the Crown to get assistance from Patrick Armstrong.'

However, the question of Armstrong's participation was not as Bevan, the defence or the judge presented it to the jury: Armstrong not only never refused to appear in court, he had never been invited.

In February 1990, three months after his release, Armstrong was asked to attend an interview by officers from the Sharples team who wrote to Alastair Logan, Armstrong's solicitor. The officers did not specify what they wanted to interview Armstrong about, and there was no mention of Attwell, Donaldson and Style. Logan replied, saying the request had come at a difficult time for his client, who had only recently been released after fifteen years in prison. Logan added that Armstrong was suffering from post-traumatic stress and was being treated by Dr James MacKeith, a consultant forensic psychiatrist. The request for an interview, Logan told the Sharples team, would be referred to MacKeith. On 30 March 1990 Logan told the officers that Armstrong was willing to be interviewed, and that he (Logan) was merely waiting for the view of the doctor. Logan repeated the substance of this on 12 April 1990 to Detective Chief Superintendent Peter Brock, who was in operational charge of the Sharples team. Two weeks later, MacKeith set out the conditions he considered necessary for such an interview so as to safeguard the health of his patient. MacKeith requested that the interview be videoed, that it be held in familiar surroundings, that Logan and MacKeith be present throughout, and that Armstrong be able to rest or terminate the interview at his own request. Such conditions may be out of the usual run of things, but they are common in cases in which the victim has been severely traumatized. Jim Sharples, by then Chief Constable of Merseyside, rejected MacKeith's conditions in a letter to Logan in May 1990.

Two weeks later Logan again wrote to Sharples, emphasizing

that Armstrong was willing to be interviewed. Logan made similar assurances to the then DPP, Sir Allan Green. In July Anne Butler of the Crown Prosecution Service replied on behalf of Allan Green, saying that the CPS had discussed the matter with Brock and that she hoped there might still be an amicable solution. Logan then received a questionnaire from the Sharples team to which Armstrong was asked to reply. Logan complained to the DPP that the questions were 'in the most general of terms', that they did not relate to any of the documents that formed the basis of the decision by the DPP not to defend the 1989 appeal, and that he was being placed in the invidious position of having to interview his own client without knowing to what use any resulting information might be put. Logan told the DPP that it wasn't his function but that of the police to conduct such interviews. During September and October Logan wrote further letters in which he insisted that Armstrong was willing to be interviewed under the conditions MacKeith had laid down. After October 1990, however, neither the DPP nor the Sharples team made any further effort to interview Armstrong. It is worth noting that all the correspondence took place before charges were brought against the detectives, and that once proceedings had begun there was no further attempt to enlist Armstrong.

When asked why, in the interests of justice, he didn't just throw his hands up and say to his client, 'Forget the conditions, go to court,' Logan replies that he couldn't go against Mac-Keith's advice. Armstrong was MacKeith's patient, he had undergone an appalling experience and needed care and treatment. But Logan emphatically rejects the suggestion that his client ever 'refused' to give evidence. He goes further: if, as Lawson and the other barristers for the defence asserted during the trial of the three detectives, Armstrong was so important to the defendants' case, why did they not seek to subpoena him to force him to appear in court? This was a course open to them, and there would have been no difficulty in contacting

Armstrong, who has recently been living in Dublin but who travels regularly back and forth to London. As it was, the defence was allowed to imply that Armstrong was absent because he – rather than the former detectives – had something to hide.

If Bevan felt no need either to put the record straight or to defend Armstrong's innocence, the defence felt no compunction about asserting his guilt. On the second day of the trial Lawson told the court that when arrested Armstrong 'sang like a canary' about his involvement in the IRA; Armstrong had been 'falling over himself to give information'. Lawson asked the jury:

> Did he confess and if so on what terms? It is impossible for common sense to avoid asking: if he did confess, why? The answer to 'why?' can only be either because it was true or because, as was asserted on his behalf at his trial, he was forced to confess through the use of threats and some actual violence.

The possibility that he had been intimidated had been considered and rejected by the jury in 1975, Lawson continued, 'and they had the advantage of hearing from Patrick Armstrong.' If the confessions were true, he asked, why should his client and his two co-accused lie about the contemporaneous notes? 'Why fabricate the truth?'

If there is a single phrase by which the proceedings in Court Eight will be remembered it is Lawson's 'Why fabricate the truth?' By adopting this line of defence – a line which surely Bevan expected – Lawson was making Armstrong's supposed guilt (and that of Paul Hill and Gerry Conlon; Carole Richardson, interestingly, was largely ignored in the proceedings) central to the defence case. As the trial progressed, the defence became bolder in their assertions about Armstrong. Careful at first to avoid saying directly that he was guilty, by the time it came to the closing speeches all inhibitions had been shed.

Anthony Evans QC, for Donaldson, asked the jury: 'Can anyone believe that Armstrong was not an active member of the IRA?' He continued:

> We say to you that the innocent Patrick Armstrong does not exist. He is a media creation, a creation of the ill-informed, the misinformed and those who do not want to be informed . . . Can anyone who has been in this court not believe that he was responsible for the Guildford bombings?

Elsewhere in his address Evans referred to 'the so-called innocent Guildford Four'. Anthony Glass QC, for Style, said simply: 'Armstrong was the bomb carrier.' It was all to underline the defence contention that the detectives had no need to fabricate evidence because Armstrong was guilty and had freely confessed.

Contrary to the impression the defence barristers were seeking to create, there had never been any question about the fact that Armstrong had confessed, and confessed . . . and confessed. He confessed while under police interrogation, during his remand, and, like Conlon, post-conviction. In legal proceedings confessions are always important. Hill, Conlon, Armstrong and Richardson were convicted solely and exclusively on the basis of their confessions. There was no other evidence of any kind. Thus, the issue of why and what they confessed has always been utterly crucial – in the 1975 trial, the 1977 and 1989 appeals, and in the trial of the three former detectives, during which it was suggested time and again that the confessions were definitive proof of the Four's guilt. Why did Armstrong, Hill, Conlon and Richardson confess? Over the years I have spoken to many people about the Guildford case. Even those prepared to believe that miscarriages of justices do occur found it difficult to understand why a person would admit to crimes he has not committed. Michael Fisher, Hill's solicitor after 1987, was initially far from convinced of his new client's innocence. 'If he is innocent,' Fisher said to me, 'why did he confess?' Fisher could not understand.

In 1974, only a few weeks before the arrest that was to change Paddy Armstrong's life for ever, my own life took a sudden turn for the worse. I was charged with murder; the man I was accused of murdering was a police inspector, shot dead in the course of a brief gunfight during an IRA bank robbery near Belfast. In view of the seriousness of the situation, in view of what was to happen to me subsequently, I find it odd that what I remember most vividly about the moment of my arrest – at one in the morning – was the fact that the men surrounding me were large and adult. That they were armed RUC detectives and had come for me and my brother (who was a year my junior) seemed, at the time, to weigh less with me than the fact of their size and age. Until that night, I had known little of the world of adult men. Some disagreement between my parents had led to my brother and me being brought up by our mother. Our wider family was dominated by aunts, not uncles, by grandmothers, not grandfathers, and my childhood and adolescence had been shaped by the sight and sound of these Belfast women. The men I knew were not men, properly speaking, but my contemporaries, lads. In the doorway of our flat, at the moment of my arrest, I found myself thinking about age and size, and the discrepancy in our relative positions. I was slightly built, they were not; they knew what this was about, I did not. They were studying me, and it was evident they were not impressed. I was a suspect in the killing of a colleague of theirs. They were not neutral about me. I was at once frightened and fascinated by their manner. More than anything else, they seemed powerful. They had cars and radios and guns. They carried themselves in a way that took for granted some kind of precedence; these men expected to be noticed and obeyed. I do not like to admit it now, but though I was nervous, I was also most definitely impressed. I do not like to admit it because I have, in the intervening years, been in the company of many men like them and I realize now that they are often a great deal less imposing seen at closer quarters and from a less disadvantageous point of view. I can look back now and see that most of those involved in my arrest were of average intelligence, no more than that, that not a few were bigoted, and two were simple thugs.

In the police station, even as I was thinking that this shouldn't take long to clear up, I could also hear other thoughts at work: you are in serious trouble; these men don't like you and they don't believe you. These anxieties stemmed only in part from the nature and seriousness of their allegations, more from having been brought up in a particular environment at a particular time. I understood the RUC to be Protestant, pro-Unionist and suspicious of young Catholic men; I was 18, Catholic, anti-Unionist and nervous of Protestant men with guns. I had another anxiety: they had also arrested my brother. Somewhere in the same building he was being interrogated. When I asked about him, I was assured he would be well treated. One of my interrogators said: You will have heard stories about police brutality, they are not true, neither you nor your brother will be abused or harmed. Nevertheless, I was anxious, for myself, for my brother. So when questioned about what the police call a suspect's 'antecedents' (background) I was helpful, amenable, informative; more so than I would normally care to be. I realized that I was trying to please. It took no great insight on my part to sense the anger massing just below the surface of these men. I did not want to spark it by saying or doing anything that could be interpreted by them as a less than whole-hearted desire to comply. Thus I found myself giving out those awful, humiliating signs of compliance – the weak laughs and smiles, the subliminal signals saying I accept you have power over me, you are more important than me. When one officer passed comment on the neatness of my handwriting compared with his, I said his wasn't so bad, and we gave each other a smile: mine only just not quite craven, his thin with loathing ill-concealed. More important, when I asked to see a solicitor and was told that only those with something to hide wanted a lawyer present, I gave in without complaint. The boundaries of what was permissible in this special place were entirely of their creation; I would be wise not to try to test them, or the patience of the men who patrolled them.

The first interrogation did not last more than a couple of hours; it was not violent, nor was it even particularly frightening. When it was over, I was moved for a couple of hours' sleep to another police station. Except I did not sleep. The next day I asked about my brother and was told that he was cracking up, and they asked me if he had a history of mental problems. He hadn't; I said I did not believe them. They said they didn't care what I believed but it was true. There was now a hardness, an edge, about their attitude to me. As they drove me to an interrogation centre, one said: I'll stop the car. You get out, run. I'll give you a start of five. If you get away, fine; if I catch you I'll shoot you dead. The interrogation started again, the veneer of restraint wearing thinner. As the detectives became more aggressive, I held on to the assurance I had been given that I would not be abused. The day wore on. They told me my brother had completely cracked up, that his mind had gone. Perhaps he was the guilty one, not me. They said they were thinking of charging him. I was sitting in a chair denying that I had been involved in the bank robbery and murder while two officers circled me, firing questions. I do not now remember what I said to provoke him, but one officer stepped up to me and struck me across the face with his open hand. I said that I'd been told I would not be hit. I saw the two exchange a glance. Looking back, I interpret it as the one saying to the other: Don't, it's not working, it won't get us anywhere.

More interviews, more time in the cells alone. I had no intention of making the confession they wanted, and I felt sure I could hold out. But I was aware that perspective was slipping. No watch, no track of time, unable to distinguish between the faces of the series of men who came in and out to question me, completely in the power of these men, without even the freedom to piss when I needed to. Growing anxiety about my brother. Late in the night, the officer who had seemed to me the least aggressive – the one who had assured me I would not be abused and who had sent his colleague the silent warning after I had been struck – came to tell me that my brother's condition had deteriorated. My brother was, and remains, a gentle person: I do not remember ever having seen him in a fight, an unusual distinction in Belfast, and when I recall him from 1974 I remember his interest in Cat Stevens and T Rex, in pacifism and lilac T-shirts. I asked to see him. Only if I signed a confession. No. The questioning went on. They told me my mother was waiting outside the barracks – had been waiting since the moment of our arrest. If I signed, she could collect my brother and take him home. It was the early hours of the morning. I had had no sleep for thirty hours. I would not say what they wanted me to say.

A break in proceedings. I was left alone. There is nothing more disturbing to the suspect than these apparently random entries and exits and whispered exchanges – disturbing because they drive home the fact that your fate is being decided by others, outside your view and hearing. When they returned they said: Come, we are going to show you your brother. They took me to the cells area. They unlocked the door. My brother was squatting, unseeing and indifferent, clutching a grey army blanket around him; I could not see clearly in the penumbra of the cell, but I had the sense he was naked under the blanket. He stared at the wall and there was nothing in his eyes; he was out, and no word of mine could bring him back in. It was the most painful sight I had seen. But when the

detectives closed the cell door on my brother and said to me,
Sign and he will be released immediately, if you don't. we'll
charge him as well as you, I immediately said: Charge him.
There was a brief silence. One of the officers looked me in the
face and said: You are a cold-hearted, calculating young man.

I did not sign, I did not confess to something I hadn't done.
But what if I had said yes? My confession, what would it have
been? I knew nothing of the bank robbery, nothing of the
gunfight, nothing of the killing. What details would I have
given, could I have given? I need have had no worries, there
would have been no problem about my lack of firsthand
knowledge. The confession would have contained details
known only to the guilty party. A detective would have asked:
'Did you meet so-and-so the morning before the robbery?' I
nod. 'Did you tell him we had a job on?' Another nod or
perhaps a weak yes. 'And did you go the next day in the blue
four-door saloon to the bank? Was the car stolen earlier in the
New Lodge area? Were you carrying the sub-machine-gun and
so-and-so the pistol? Did you shoot the officer when he am-
bushed you on emerging from the bank?' Yes to the first
question, yes to the last. Yes to all of it. And in its statement
form my confession would have read: 'I met so-and-so in the
morning and told him we had a job on the next day. The car
we got was a blue four-door saloon which had been stolen
earlier in the New Lodge area. I carried the sub-machine-gun
and so-and-so had the pistol . . .' And the prosecution would
have adduced this statement in court as formidable and conclusive evidence against me, convincing because why else would
I have confessed (in the absence of any evidence of intimidation), and because it contained details which could only have
been known by someone who had been involved. And, of
course, by the detectives investigating the case.

There is an instinct, probably more pronounced in writers,
to look for set pieces: events, usually small in scale and

timespan, that turn out to have lasting and profound meaning. These set pieces also tend to be associated with change. So perhaps I exaggerate the impact of seeing my brother in that condition, in his blankness, of my refusal to sign, of the detective's words to me. But somehow that moment now seems more important than the arrest and the imprisonment which followed. I did not before then know that I was capable of making such a decision; now, certainly, I recognize in myself a tendency to the final, the fixed, and an impatience with those slow to make up their minds. The characters in fiction and drama I look for and sympathize with are those who, after whatever ordeal, make their decision, whatever the cost, and keep to it. And this set piece, this incident in half-light outside a cell in a Belfast police barracks, crystallizes the moment when I first began to understand that tendency.

I did not confess, but Paddy Armstrong did. All the evidence is that Armstrong is a passive and amenable man; 'weak-willed' and 'easily led' in the words of the more judgemental; 'suggestible' in the words of the psychiatrists. Armstrong is not an achiever, a thinker, or very much of a doer; he is, in truth, a bit of a disaster, the kind of man incapable of getting through life without constant support from family and friends; he has about him an air of something between bewilderment and trepidation, and it never seems to go away. But he is also a pleasant, gentle and well-meaning man. He is not rancorous, he harbours no grudges, and he is completely devoid of aggression. The first conversation I had with him came after a phone call from Gerry Conlon, who had travelled to Los Angeles to try to raise interest in making a film of his book *Proved Innocent*. Conlon, who shares the working-class Belfast man's congenital horror of being away from 'his own', took Armstrong along for the ride and the company. When Conlon came on the phone – at 2 a.m. London time – it was to tell me, in excited tones, of his success in Los Angeles. He had been a big hit (no mention of how Paddy had gone down). He and Paddy had just

returned from dinner with Gabriel Byrne, the Irish actor, and
Byrne's wife Ellen Barkin. After telling me at some length that
Byrne thought *Proved Innocent* 'brilliant' and was going to make
the film, Conlon said suddenly: 'Have a word with Paddy.' I
did not know Armstrong and didn't quite know what to say to
him, but I assumed that, like most Belfast people, he would be
into 'the slagging'   a (frequently rough) form of teasing. I
kidded him, gently enough, about mixing with the stars. It
was at once clear that Armstrong was awestruck. 'They
treated us really nice,' he said, wonder and gratitude in his
voice. 'And,' he went on, 'we got our picture took with Ellen.'
'Send me a copy,' I said. 'Yeah, I will.' 'But do me a favour,' I
teased him, 'cut yourself out and just send me Ellen's.' The
silence told me at once that I had hurt his feelings. When he
spoke it was to say quietly: 'That's not a very nice thing to
say.' 'Paddy, I'm sorry,' I said, 'I was only slagging.' I then
heard him say: 'Here, Gerry, you talk to him.' He was holding
the receiver at arm's length.

Everyone who knows him agrees that Armstrong is a timid
man with few resources. By his own admission, he was at the
time of his arrest in 1974 a habitual drug-user, taking anything
and everything he could lay his hands on. He lived with
motley crews in squats and abandoned houses in the Kilburn-
Cricklewood area; he signed on, shoplifted food from super-
markets, and fantasized with his friends about 'big scores'. It
was a desultory life at best, and one to which young working-
class men from Ireland seem all too susceptible on arrival in
London. They come with little idea of how to look after
themselves, for the nature of a working-class Irish upbringing
leaves most young men ill-equipped to organize anything as
complex as the shopping, the washing, the cooking or the
cleaning. Meals are fish-and-chips and kebabs, homes are
what you can break into and squat, furniture is what can be
carried out of a skip, heating is from abstracted electricity.
Drink, drugs and sex are the rewards of this kind of life, a life

captured most evocatively in the lyrics of Shane MacGowan and the Pogues — right down to the Tuinal and the beatings in police custody in MacGowan's 'Old Main Drag'. If he had come from a middle-class home, Armstrong would have been called a drop-out. As it was, he came from a background of deprivation almost unimaginable in contemporary Western Europe. Paddy Armstrong had nothing to drop out from; he was therefore called a 'dosser'. I once knew an addict who got caught in a sudden downpour, went home, turned on the oven, put in his wet feet to warm up, and fell asleep; both legs had to be amputated below the knee. I knew another addict who took his last fix by Regent's Canal in London. Armstrong could easily have ended up like either of these. In 1974 he was not a model citizen, he was not someone you would have felt happy about welcoming into your home. But then he did not go on trial for being a petty criminal, drug-user and marginal member of society: he went on trial for being an IRA bomber – and just as most of those reading this article would not have wanted to go near Armstrong in 1974, neither would the IRA. When he was arrested his clothes were unwashed, he had scabies, and he had no idea of what was going on.

Armstrong's defence has always been that he was unable to resist police abuse in Guildford. But given Armstrong's highly dependent and suggestible personality, one is tempted to speculate that, in the absence of an experienced solicitor to safeguard his interests, little if any actual violence would have been required to get him to talk. He was intimidated merely by being in the presence of authority figures (something I recognize, though in a much less severe form, from my own experience), and was desperate to ingratiate himself for fear of what the police might do next (something I also recognize). But, of course, it has always been alleged that the pressures on Armstrong and the other suspects were much greater than mere psychological violence – something the police have always hotly denied. In the police account, the arrests, detentions and interviews were carried out quite calmly. Reading their witness statements, one gets the impression of composed, disinterested professionals getting on with the job. When it comes to the detention of Paul Hill, for example, the witness statement of Detective Sergeant Anthony Jermey reads: 'Hill was conveyed to Guildford and placed in the cells.' In *Stolen Years*, this is how Hill remembers being 'placed in the cells':

> When we arrived at Guildford Police Station I was taken from the car and into the foyer. There was a crowd of uniformed officers milling around the desk waiting to get a look at me. Jermey said: 'We got the bastard.' The desk sergeant replied: 'Oh, nice one Cyril.' And that, how does that sound? To me it was more sinister than Jermey's brutish and crude threats. The officers wore hard faces. They ran me along to the cells and pushed me inside. I was searched. All the time, they kept up their threats and insults. When they had finished their search, Jermey pushed my face into the wall. He pointed to some graffiti: I think it said something like 'I love Chrissie.' 'I don't want to see any of that in here,' he shouted. They took my shoes with them when they left the cell.
>
> This is what Jermey meant when he said I was conveyed to Guildford and placed in the cells.

The following is from Conlon's account (from *Proved Innocent*) of arriving in Surrey:

> As soon as I walked through the door of Addlestone Police Station, any comforting thought about civilized Surrey was shattered ... I was bundled out and uncuffed, then taken up some steps and into a large, elongated room where all the coppers in town seemed to be waiting for me, lined up like a gauntlet-run. As Grundy pushed me forward they inspected me up and down, not like a person but an object. I heard someone murmur: 'Irish bastard.'
>
> Then a boot shot out and struck my ankle.

'Murdering Irish bastard.'

A blob of spit landed on my shirt, another foot hit my ankle a painful kick. I stumbled a little, Grundy gave me a second push and I made halting progress down the room, flinching at each kick and each insult.

Next came the interviews. This is Hill's account of one episode:

During one interrogation, Simmons [a senior officer in the case] burst in, grabbed me by the hair and dragged me along the corridor, which was lined with police officers. As he dragged me along he gave me rabbit punches in the back of the head. Some of the officers in the corridor joined in. I was pushed through two swinging fire doors and on to the stairwell. I was pushed down the stairs. Simmons pulled me up by the hair and dragged me to the door of another interview room. The fear was so intense I could hardly feel my legs and was unable to stand. I had no idea what this was leading to or where it would end. The door opened and they brought me inside. They had to support me under the arms. I saw a woman. They said: 'Is this the woman?' I shook my head and they shouted at me: 'Is this the fucking woman?' I said: 'Yes.' It turned out to be Annie Maguire, Gerry's aunt. I had never seen her before ... There were more interviews, more names, more confessions. During one interview, Simmons burst into the room. I thought he was deranged. He screamed at me: 'Who is Mrs Davey? Who the fuck is Mrs Davey, she's got you a fucking mouthpiece,' I was so frightened by his rage that I thought to myself: 'Why did they have to go and tell a solicitor, it's just made them angry.' Simmons told me that there was no way I was going to see a solicitor.

It was, in Conlon's version, to get a lot worse. He describes how he was punched, kicked, toppled out of a chair, shouted at and threatened with guns.

In the trial of the three former detectives, defence counsel –

who, when not on their feet, could be seen reading *Stolen Years*
and *Proved Innocent* – rejected the allegations of brutality and
intimidation. They cited Armstrong's failure to report his
alleged beatings to the police doctor as evidence that he had
not been assaulted, to which Armstrong replies that he saw the
doctor as one of the police. And it is certainly true that police
doctors have come in for their fair share of criticism for failing
to attend to prisoners' medical needs. In the recent case of
Leon Patterson, held in Denton Police Station in Manchester,
a police surgeon certified the prisoner as fit to attend his
scheduled court appearance, even though he had been observed for the previous twenty hours in his blood-splattered
cell rolling around naked and delirious. A solicitor for Patterson's family said the prisoner 'had been treated like an animal
for the last twenty hours of his life' – something the police
doctor did not apparently notice. After Patterson's death,
another doctor admitted fabricating data relating to tissue
samples taken from the corpse. The inquest into Patterson's
death recorded a verdict of unlawful killing. So when, in the
trial of the former detectives, Anthony Glass QC, for Style,
called the police doctor 'the first independent, friendly face
Armstrong had seen since he was arrested', he was making
large assumptions.

We will never know exactly what went on in the different
Surrey police stations used to detain the many Guildford
suspects in November and December 1974. The police have a
vested interest in denying that any brutality took place; the
Guildford Four have reasons to exaggerate the extent of any
violence that may have occurred. But assume for a moment
that there was no violence, that the Guildford suspects were
treated with the same consideration and restraint with which
the three former detectives were treated; assume they were not
intimidated, abused or threatened. There remains enough
evidence about the manner in which at least some of the

confessions were obtained to throw doubt on their accuracy and validity. It is agreed by all that at least one of Hill's interviews was conducted in breach of the Judges' Rules, and it is now known that Armstrong had, the day before his arrest, taken a large quantity of speed and of the barbiturate Tuinal. No allowance was made for this at the time of the interrogation, and no evidence was heard on the subject in the 1975 trial. Conlon was suffering from a kidney infection, for which he received no treatment even though a police doctor had prescribed penicillin. More significantly, there is evidence to suggest that Carole Richardson may have made her first confession only after Kasimir Makos, a police surgeon, gave her an injection of 50 mg of Pethidine. This was what Makos, in 1987, told Dr James MacKeith, the forensic psychiatrist who was then assisting Alastair Logan, Richardson's solicitor. Makos's evidence was published in *Time Bomb*, the book on the Guildford and Maguire cases by Grant McKee and Ros Franey. McKee and Franey point out that there is no mention anywhere in the official record of the Pethidine injection. They quote Makos as saying that, after the injection, Richardson

> calmed down. Her agitation subsided, she ceased crying and after a cigarette smoke she appeared completely calm, composed and very reasonable. It was then she volunteered to confess to me about the bombing incident . . . I was, listening to her story, under the impression she treated the whole affair [as a] slight prank! . . . There was something weird in her confession and I was almost convinced that she did not realize the meaning of the tragedy nor was she aware of it.

Makos speculated about her motives for confessing. 'Was it my sympathetic approach to her in the cell? Was it the relief she experienced after the Pethidine injection, which appeared to suit her very well? Or was it just the total confusion of a drug addict?' The significance of Makos's evidence was obvious to the defence. If Richardson was under the influence of Pethidine

at the time of her interrogation, could her confession stand?
The significance was also appreciated by the Sharples team.
Towards the end of 1988, Superintendent Brock visited the
doctor, by then living in retirement in Belgium. After the visit,
Makos retracted what he had told MacKeith about the Pethidine injection. The Court of Appeal did not hear any evidence
on the matter, and so the issue remains unresolved. What is
not in dispute, however, is that Richardson was undergoing
withdrawal symptoms from having taken LSD. Like Armstrong, she was in a position in which she was particularly
vulnerable to suggestion. Common sense surely indicates that
any information elicited in such circumstances be treated cau-
tiously. Evidently this was not something that occurred to the
police.

If there is a single example that demonstrates beyond question the capacity of suspects to make false confessions it is that
of Judith Ward. In 1974 Ward was arrested and interviewed
about a horrific act of carnage – the murder of twelve people,
including two children, in the M62 coach bombing. Ward, a
lonely young woman with serious mental difficulties, was in
fact a serial confessor. She had previously been detained and
questioned by the RUC, who had had the sense to realize that
she was unstable and that her confessions were fantasies. Back
in England, however, detectives listening to her admissions to
a series of (completely separate) offences discounted the advice
of the RUC and ignored literally thousands of statements
pointing to her innocence. These statements were withheld
from the defence in the same way that crucial material was
kept from the Guildford Four's lawyers. The detectives might
have guessed something was amiss after members of Chipper-
field's Circus (in which Ward had worked) came forward to
say that Ward had been with them at the time of one particular
incident to which Ward had admitted in lively detail. But
instead of standing back and taking a fresh look at their
prisoner, the detectives simply struck that incident off their list

and proceeded to the next – for which, unfortunately, there were no independent witnesses. On the strength of her uncorroborated confessions, Ward was sentenced to life imprisonment. She was freed by the Court of Appeal in June last year, after eighteen years in prison, when conclusive evidence of her innocence was uncovered. Those who whisper about the Guildford Four and Birmingham Six never say anything about Judith Ward. Gareth Peirce, who acts for Ward as well as Conlon, suggests that this is because there was a full hearing before the Court of Appeal in which all the evidence of official wrongdoing was exposed. It may also be to do with the fact that Ward, like Carole Richardson – about whom Bevan and the defence lawyers were similarly reticent – is English. After Ward's release the Assistant Chief Constable of West Yorkshire, the force responsible for her imprisonment, said publicly: 'I wish to express regret, on behalf of the force, that Miss Ward has spent so many years in prison for offences ... she did not commit.'

You do not have to have mental problems to make false confessions, or be a drug addict. Or even be Irish. Roger Cooper confessed to being a British spy in Tehran after an interrogation during which he was threatened and beaten. In the same way that Armstrong invented details about the IRA to satisfy his captors, Cooper invented a spy-ring. To populate it, he says, he invented characters and gave them names from Evelyn Waugh novels. In filling out his 'bald and unconvincing narrative', Cooper was drawing on the cultural resources available to a public-school-educated, middle-class Englishman. To Cooper's surprise, his interrogators found his invented account of the inner workings of British Intelligence convincing. Armstrong's cultural references were very limited – in fact, they were restricted to drink, drugs and gambling – but he drew on them in the same way as Cooper did on his. To Armstrong's surprise, his interrogators found his account of the inner workings of the IRA (by no means as full as Cooper's equivalent

effort) convincing. Like Armstrong, Cooper repeated his confession at a later time when there was no suggestion of intimidation or violence. On reiterating to camera what he had told
his interrogators, Cooper says that he felt confident that at a
later hearing 'I would be able to explain that my confession
was false and made under duress . . . I could probably lace the
television confession with misinformation, as I had done with
the written confession, and the Iranians would end up looking
foolish internationally.' Here Cooper's motivation and ration-
ale echo something of the thinking described at different times
by each of the Guildford Four: the confessions were so obviously false, so clearly ridiculous, that they would be laughed
out of court when subjected to dispassionate analysis by an
impartial tribunal. (It is worth noting that Judith Ward continued to repeat the substance of her confessions for several
years after she was convicted.)

Even more important than how and why the Guildford Four
came to confess is what they started saying once they began.
Each made several statements. No two statements given by the
same suspect contained the same version of events; no two
statements given by two or more suspects corresponded in
anything other than a few of the most general points. The
confessions are internally inconsistent and contradicted by
many of the known facts. There are more than a hundred
discrepancies between the confessions of each of the four. They
give different personnel; different numbers in the gang; different times of departure from London; different drivers (indeed,
Armstrong was named as a driver though he did not then
know how to drive: in 1974 Belfast men from his background
rarely had access to cars); different sizes of bombs; different
containers for the bombs; different places in which the bombs
were primed; different persons taking the bombs into the pubs.
Armstrong confessed to parking the car outside the Wimpey
Bar in the High Street, which would have been impossible: it

was a pedestrian precinct. He then changed his account and said he parked in Mill Lane. This was almost as unlikely, for parking was prohibited in Mill Lane, the sides of which were painted with double yellow lines. Logan says that not only would a car parked there have quickly caused a build-up of traffic, but – given the amount of time the bombers spent in the pub – the driver would also very likely have got a ticket. Carole Richardson confessed to going into both the Seven Stars and the Horse and Groom (physically impossible, as the Crown conceded, given the timings). Each of the Four implicated not only each other but many others, three of whom were charged: Paul Colman, John McGuinness and Brian Anderson. These three did not make any incriminating statements and were released before the trial because of lack of evidence, but the detectives' barristers in Court Eight could just as easily have been talking about the 'so-called innocent Guildford Seven'.

The police say the suspects were either deliberately misleading their interviewers, having been trained in IRA anti-interrogation techniques (if they were, why did they say anything at all? Why not stay silent and be released for lack of evidence?); or they were seeking at first to minimize their own involvement and culpability. During the trial of the three former detectives, Bevan, for the Crown, said that these inconsistencies suggested that 'this was not a case in which the police had browbeaten suspects': had the police done so, the statements would have been coherent. Yet there is another and more obvious explanation for the inconsistencies: the four young people making the confessions knew nothing of the bombings. In *Stolen Years* there is a passage in which Hill gives some clues about how his confessions came to be so inaccurate:

> I admitted to bombing the King's Arms in Woolwich. I was confronted with Gerry and Paddy. Yes, they were the ones, they were all involved. Gerry and Paddy started making statements.

Because they knew nothing of the details surrounding the bombings they made things up to placate the interrogating officers. The accounts I had given conflicted with what Gerry said; what Gerry said was at odds with what Paddy told them. Carole gave a different version again ... after the different interrogating teams compared notes and saw the discrepancies they determined to have them reconciled. They would burst into the interview room and would scream: 'What you've said isn't what Conlon's saying. Start again, and this time it better tally with what Conlon has told us.'

So it would start over again. What colour was the car? Who was Marion? Who went to which pub? Who made the bombs? Where were they made? From time to time a detective would appear at the door and there would be whispered conversations. Then the interrogating officers would say to me, 'Armstrong says it was like this' or 'Conlon says it was like that.' And I would agree. Anything to stop the madness.

In the 1975 trial, one officer said most of the statements could be regarded as 'fairy-tales ... a mixture of fact and fiction'. This mixture presented Sir Michael Havers, who led for the Crown, with grave difficulties. McKee and Franey have demonstrated in *Time Bomb* how Havers negotiated these by the simple expedient of accepting what corresponded with the known facts as true and rejecting what didn't as 'deliberately misleading'. Thus, when Carole Richardson, supplied with a blank diagram of the Horse and Groom interior, marked the position of the bomb, she did so, Havers said, with 'startling accuracy'. Her two earlier stabs at it, which she got wrong, were 'deliberately misleading'. Havers also rejected Richardson's confession to having bombed both pubs. Similarly, when the police drove Hill and Conlon (separately) around the Surrey countryside and told them to point out where the bombs had been primed, the two men identified different locations: they were being deliberately misleading.

Barry Irving, the director of the Police Foundation, an independent body which conducts research into police practice, has analysed the confessions. He begins by saying: 'Interrogation ... is a two-way process in which the participants swap information. The interrogator lets the suspect know what he wants to find out, when he is dissatisfied with answers, where he requires extra detail, when he wants to understand connections between statements, what he believes or disbelieves and what his attitudes to the information are.' Of Armstrong's confessions, Irving says: 'the police statements show that Armstrong was heavily coached by his interrogators.' Alastair Logan has put the same point more colourfully: 'If Armstrong sang like a canary, it was a song the police had taught him.' What is incontestable is that the confessions made by Hill, Conlon, Armstrong and Richardson did not contain any detail about the bombings that was not then known to the police.

So it was that the issue of the confessions – and of Armstrong's confessions in particular – came to dominate the trial of Attwell, Donaldson and Style, the defence making hay with them and the prosecution apparently reluctant to do anything to spoil their fun. But, of course, the real issue before the jury was not the confessions: it was whether the manuscript notes of the three interviews with Armstrong had been made contemporaneously. Bevan reminded the jury that Lawson had asked: 'Why fabricate the truth?' The answer, he said, was simple: 'to bolster your evidence to ensure you are believed.' He might also have added – but didn't – that if a suspect has been threatened and abused during interrogation, a certain amount of rewriting will obviously be required: the answers can usually stay the same but the questions will have to be rephrased.

What, then, was the evidence to show that the rough typed notes had been a draft for the manuscript? Bevan told the jury it was 'essentially an inference case ... there is no direct evidence available to the Crown to prove the manuscript notes were not contemporaneous.' Instead, Bevan's case rested on a

comparison between the rough typed notes and the manuscript
notes.

Bevan started with examples of small differences. In the
rough typed notes, Armstrong is reported at one point as
saying: 'In 1969 when I joined [the IRA] I did it in Dundalk.
I don't know where.' The words 'I don't know where' do not
appear in the 'contemporaneous' manuscript note. Why not?
Because, Bevan suggested, it was a bit like having a barrister
say: 'I did my last case at the Old Bailey. I don't know where.'
The form in the rough typed notes was suggestive of someone
unfamiliar with Irish geography: an English person, a Surrey
detective perhaps, might think Dundalk was a region or county
rather than a small market town. The 'I don't know where'
reflects this lack of knowledge. A Belfast man like Armstrong
would know exactly what and where Dundalk was. Conse-
quently, when it came to putting the polished version together,
the last words were cut.

Elsewhere, Bevan said, the omission of words and phrases in
the rough typed notes from the manuscript version reflected
the three officers' anxiety about being accused of oppression
and breaches of the Judges' Rules. Thus the words 'I only
want the truth' and 'Now tell us the truth', which appear in
the rough typed notes but not in the manuscript, could have
been removed in anticipation of later defence challenges on
grounds of oppression. These challenges could have led to
certain questions, and even whole passages, being ruled inadmissible; something the officers, in making up the manuscript,
would obviously have wanted to avoid.

There were also, Bevan continued, examples of *non sequiturs*
in the rough typed notes that do not appear in the manuscript
version. These were rewritten to make the questioning sound
more authentic. More damagingly, Bevan pointed to passages
of some length that appear in the rough typed notes but not in
the manuscript. For example: 'Now Connolly is Conlon, the
man that has been arrested. Is that right?' These thirteen words

appear in the rough typed notes but not in the manuscript. How, Bevan asked, could Attwell – if he was typing up his own notes. notes which, it must be remembered, he claims were made contemporaneously – have inserted thirteen extra words into the rough typed notes? Bevan pointed to another passage of fifty-five words in the rough typed notes, not one word of which appears in the manuscript note. How could Attwell and the others 'remember' a passage of fifty-five words after the interview if they were making the typed notes from a contemporaneous record of the interview? And there was another passage – of 101 words – in the rough typed notes, missing from the supposedly contemporaneous notes. In a further passage in the manuscript notes the phrasing is changed in such a way as to suggest that Armstrong mentioned the name of John McGuinness of his own accord; in the rough typed notes the police are the first to mention McGuinness's name.

The jury didn't hear that a similar alteration had been discovered in one of Hill's interviews: the change implied that Hill had voluntarily implicated Richardson, whereas in the original version Hill was responding to his interrogators' suggestion. The rough typed notes also contained alterations in the sequence of the questioning and there were arrows to indicate that certain passages be reordered.

The most compelling part of Bevan's comparison exercise related to the rough typed notes of an interview in which an entire sequence was moved. The sequence dealt with an interview conducted with Armstrong on 4 December which began at 11.50 a.m. At the same time as Armstrong was being questioned, an acquaintance of his, Paul Colman, whom Armstrong had implicated in the Guildford bombings, was under interrogation in a different room in Guildford Police Station. Armstrong's interrogating officers wanted what the police call a 'confrontation' so that Armstrong could identify Colman. Detective Chief Inspector John Horton, one of the team questioning Colman, brought Colman to the room in which

Armstrong was being interviewed. Armstrong identified Colman and a brief exchange followed. In the rough typed notes the confrontation is recorded as taking place at 1.15 p.m. The word 'move' appears beside the confrontation. In Court Eight, Bevan argued that Attwell, Donaldson and Style had to move the entire sequence further back in the notes because it came after only six pages of questions and answers. Since there were only twenty-two pages for the entire interview (which lasted 145 minutes, an average of six and a half minutes per page), the confrontation came in the rough typed notes version approximately forty minutes into the interview. This would have been at 12.30 p.m. In order to allow for the extra 45 minutes Attwell, Donaldson and Style, Bevan suggested, had to alter the sequence of the interview. They moved the confrontation back when Attwell copied out the manuscript notes. The wording used during the confrontation was also changed: the rough typed notes and the manuscript gave two different versions.

Bevan seemed only to appreciate the significance of one of the amendments in the rough typed notes at a late stage, and in the jury's absence, during protracted legal argument at the close of the prosecution case. He could have made more of the point. Again, it had to do with Paul Colman. In addition to implicating him in Guildford, Armstrong had told Attwell, Donaldson and Style that Colman had robbed a chemist's shop in Belsize Park in order to steal drugs. Colman was then in another room in Guildford Police Station being interrogated by Detective Chief Inspector John Horton. It is agreed by all the officers concerned that the information about the robbery originated with Armstrong during an interview on 4 December 1974. According to Attwell's manuscript notes, Armstrong first made his allegation about Colman and the robbery at 2.25 p.m. However, in Horton's version of events he had cautioned Colman and begun to question him about the robbery at 1.12 p.m. In Bevan's words: 'Mr Horton was relying on information from Patrick Armstrong about the chemist's job before Armstrong had even uttered a word about it.' The discrepancy was strongly suggestive of the 'contemporaneous' manuscript note having been written up after the interview. Attwell, Donaldson and Style would have been questioned about their notes and about how Horton got to know of the robbery had Lawson not objected on the grounds that Bevan had failed to call any evidence – specifically, DCI Horton – on this point and was now trying to introduce it by the back door. The judge agreed with Lawson, ruled the robbery issue inadmissible and Bevan lost a piece of evidence which, had it been heard, could well have given the case an additional twist.

At the end of his exercise in comparison, Bevan said: 'On a draft you would expect to find changes and deletions and amendments, which is precisely what you get in the rough typed notes.' The amendments indicated changes of mind among the three defendants as they were preparing their polished versions. The alterations were intended to avoid any possible hint of oppression, to make the phrasing more consistent, and to avoid being caught out over timings. If this was the case the police were probably using 'trigger' notes – rough notes taken during the interviews from which they refreshed their memory when the rough typed notes were being prepared. They then read over the typed version, made their alterations, and copied the result out by hand. This – the comparison between the two sets of documents – was the evidence on which Bevan rested his case. If it did not seem exactly overwhelming, it still threw up certain doubts about the officers and what they had been up to: specifically, what were the rough typed notes for, if they weren't used as a draft for the manuscript notes? What would the officers say in their own defence?

The right to silence is a cornerstone of the British legal system. At least that is one point of view. Another – shared by the police, by Kenneth Clarke and by Sir Hugh Annesley, the Chief Constable of Northern Ireland – is that it is outmoded and favours the guilty, and should be scrapped because it is routinely exploited by clever criminals and terrorists. (Annesley has even suggested that refusal to answer police questions should be made an offence.) The three police officers in this case had already taken advantage of the right to silence once before the trial – in the summer of 1990 when they were interviewed by members of the Sharples team. Now in Court Eight of the Old Bailey they took advantage of it again. It would be unfair, the defence argued, to subject the defendants to questioning about events that happened so long ago. But this was not to say they did not have a defence. In August 1990, the barristers went on, the three officers had, through their solicitor, given the police signed statements setting out their position. They adamantly denied they had acted improperly and said that after such a long time they could not remember why the rough typed notes had been prepared. Attwell speculated that they might have been made for internal police intelligence documents – reports of what Armstrong had said in his interviews which could then be pooled for general use in the inquiry. Or they might have been used in applications for detention under the Prevention of Terrorism Act. Or to assist the civilian typist when it came to preparing the police witness statements. Anticipating the obvious challenge that, if such information was needed for pooling in an urgent and ongoing inquiry it could simply be photocopied, Attwell said in his signed statement that his handwriting was poor and the state of photocopying in 1974 was not what it is today. Donaldson and Style signed statements to the same effect. The officers were adamant: there had to be an innocent explanation for the rough typed notes – but they couldn't remember it.

Bevan had copies of the officers' signed statements and knew of the 'photocopier' defence, but he decided to call no evidence to challenge their somewhat vague claims about the state of photocopying in 1974. (It was not disputed that there was a photocopier in the newly built and equipped Guildford Police Station.) For the purposes of this article I put in two calls. The first was to Toshiba, whose machines in 1974 were distributed through Lion Office Equipment. The man from Toshiba told me that copy quality in 1974 was 'perfectly good': if today's quality were to be marked ten out of ten, 1974's would get 'eight, maybe slightly more'. The main innovations, the man from Toshiba went on to tell me, have taken place in the way adjustments are made in the toner/developer mix. In 1974 this was done mechanically, by the operator, rather than electronically as it is now. If one were copying, say, a hundred pages the first eighty or so would come out well, after that the toner/developer mix might require some simple manual readjustment to avoid 'background build-up'. A call to The Copier People elicited the information that the main difference between today's photocopier technology and that of 1974 was in the replacement of the 'cold pressure bonding system' which in the old days 'used to make the paper go all shiny and horrible', but 'apart from that the copies were perfectly legible'. It's not much fun to read about photocopier technology (it's not much fun to write about it), but Bevan might have wanted to question a point raised repeatedly during the trial in the defendants' favour and which went entirely unchallenged. It is harder to comment on Attwell's handwriting (I didn't get to see it: crime beat reporters and legal correspondents were denied sight of the case papers, a rare – very rare – occurrence) except that it seemed to deteriorate during the course of the trial: early on it was merely 'difficult to read'; it progressed, or rather regressed, to 'thoroughly illegible and ill-formed' in Glass's closing speech.

We are on firmer ground in testing some of the other hypotheses advanced by Attwell, Donaldson and Style in their signed statements. As to their claim that the rough typed notes might have been prepared for use as 'internal information

documents', none of the witnesses involved in the Guildford
investigation came forward to say they remembered having
seen them. Passage of time, perhaps. But then Sir Peter Imbert,
the former Metropolitan Commissioner, stepped up to the
witness-box. In 1974 Imbert had been investigating the Woolwich bombing, to which Hill and Armstrong made confessions
while in Guildford Police Station. Imbert is an organized man.
He has excellent shorthand, and he holds on to and files
everything. But not even he could remember having seen the
rough typed notes or anything like them. It might have been
thought that, if the typed notes were made for internal intelligence purposes, they would have informed Imbert of Armstrong's supposed involvement in Woolwich. As it was, Imbert
found out about the content of Armstrong's confessions apparently without the assistance of Attwell's typed notes. (After
Bevan suggested that the rough typed notes were too full to
have been an internal document – they included even the full
form of the caution against self-incrimination, something 'every
policeman in the land knows by heart' – the defence pointed
out that Attwell was not the brightest of men and would have
been incapable of making a reliable précis.) Nor did any of the
civilian typists working in Guildford Police Station in 1974
come to court to give evidence to support the officers' claim
that the rough typed notes might have been used to assist
them in the preparation of the police witness statements. The
failure to find support for their line of defence might be
thought to be suggestive of guilt. But, Mr Justice Macpherson
warned the jury in his summing up, that would be a mistaken
inference. 'It is negative evidence,' he told them, which could
not be held against the officers.

Attwell explained the amendments and deletions in the
rough typed notes as mistakes. They were not sinister. They
came about because he was 'not a trained copy-typist'. He was
typing quickly and the emphasis was on speed rather than
accuracy. (Again, it wasn't clear why there had been no resort

to the photocopier.) Such 'enhancements' as existed in the rough typed notes came about because during the typing he, Donaldson and Style remembered things Attwell had not had time to record in the contemporaneous notes. Neither he nor his co-accused had ever said the manuscript was a verbatim contemporaneous record. Anthony Evans QC, for Donaldson, stressed what the judge agreed was a strong point in favour of the defence: the rough typed notes had been kept in Armstrong's 'personal file' along with the other case papers in an office in Guildford Police Station. That office was none other than the one used by his client, Detective Sergeant John Donaldson, until his retirement five years earlier. If the notes had been sinister, why had Donaldson not destroyed them? It was a point raised time and again by the defence and by the judge. A fair point. Bevan could only venture that the officers had simply forgotten their existence. The defence countered that one forgets the norm, one remembers the abnormal. These officers would never have forgotten something as abnormal as fabricated documents. But the existence of a much larger body of suspect documents in the Guildford case – material which was not brought to the attention of this jury – might suggest that the rough typed notes, if faked, were not necessarily abnormal.

Here it is worth detouring briefly into police culture and practice. What was the norm in 1974? It is well established that during the early seventies corruption was rife in the Metropolitan Police. The standard work on this is *The Fall of Scotland Yard* by Barry Cox, John Shirley and Martin Short. These and other journalists uncovered a pattern of casual and widespread corruption among officers of all ranks. Sir Robert Mark, the Metropolitan Commissioner at the time, was determined to root out the 'bad apples'. In February 1976 Mark announced that 82 officers had been dismissed following formal proceedings; a further 301 had left voluntarily during the course of criminal or disciplinary inquiries; 46 were currently suspended, 10 of them awaiting trial, 24 awaiting the decision of the DPP, and the remaining 12 subject to internal disciplinary inquiries. Most of these men had been accused of being 'bent for themselves', taking bribes from criminals to suppress evidence, and skimming off profits from drugs, prostitution and other rackets.

In this respect the Met may have been dirtier than other forces. Being 'bent for the job', on the other hand, was not something confined to the Met. Charles Pollard, Chief Constable of Thames Valley, recently told the BBC's *Panorama* that at one time 'there was a lot of scope to manipulate the system.' Keith Hellawell, Chief Constable of West Yorkshire, said on the same programme that suspects were physically frightened of detectives, though officers tended to use that perception rather than violence itself. Criticized by junior officers for comments 'damaging to the reputation of the police', the new Metropolitan Commissioner Paul Condon, who had also taken part in the programme, replied: 'I think there was a time when the majority of officers were prepared to bend the rules. I think they were prepared to massage the evidence, not for their own gain, but elaborating on things that were said to make sure that the case had the strongest chance of going through to conviction.' Sir Robert Mark, the terror of those who were bent for themselves, says in his autobiography:

> Let me make it quite clear that I am one of those who believe that if the criminal law and the procedures relating to it were applied strictly according to the book, as a means of protecting society it would collapse within a few days. There has long been an unwillingness in this country to define police powers. Rather has the tendency been to expect the police to run the risk of criticism or worse in dealing with suspected criminals.

Mark acknowledged that suspects were often abused during their detention:

There was a willingness by the police to use violence against the hardened criminal which I believe now to be rare indeed, and perhaps more important, strongly disapproved of by most policemen if ever it does occur.

In the forties, however, policing was still a fairly rough and tough business. I can remember a very successful, fairly senior detective in Manchester, who, when dealing with hardened criminals, had his own version of the Judges' Rules. It consisted of greeting the prisoner with the blunt inquiry, 'Will you talk or be tanned?' If the reply was in the negative, sometimes colourfully so, the prisoner was removed smartly to the lavatory where he was upended and his head jammed down the bowl. It usually took two to hold him, whilst a third repeatedly pulled the chain until a waggling of the feet indicated a more compliant attitude. He then signed a form headed by the usual caution against self-incrimination . . . practices such as this were perfectly well known to solicitors, to counsel, to judges and to the Press but no one did anything about them because there seemed no obvious way to achieve a fair balance between the public interest and the rights of wrongdoers.

Although senior police officers always maintain that these are the practices of the bad old days and long since abandoned, there is sufficient evidence from the eighties and nineties to suggest that while some of the scope for police wrongdoing has been reduced by the Police and Criminal Evidence Act, the problem of being bent for the job has not disappeared. One only has to read Denis Campbell's reports in *Time Out*, and Duncan Campbell's in the *Guardian*, to know that serious police wrongdoing persists. And one only has to read Roger Graef's *Talking Blues* and Robert Chesshyre's *The Force: Inside the Police*, in which serving police officers talk frankly about themselves and the job, to understand that the propensity to 'enhance' evidence against men the police genuinely believe to be guilty has not diminished. Here is Graef on the subject:

'Fitting up' – framing people on false charges or evidence – has long been a part of police folklore. There is no doubt that the practice has gone on, sometimes on a widespread scale. Although some detectives have fitted up suspects for corrupt reasons, in order to drop false charges in exchange for money, many police officers have done it with good intentions, as it were. The pressure to produce better results, often coupled with a genuine desire to see justice done, encourages officers to fit up people whom they fear might otherwise escape punishment or who are 'due' for a conviction, having evaded it for previous crimes. Where evidence is lacking, it is sometimes planted. Interviews produce 'confessions' supported by perjury on the witness-stand, often with a number of officers involved.

Graef quotes a constable in a large Northern urban force in a case of 'verbals': 'One of the magistrates actually said, Well, it's very hard for this court to believe that the PCs, the Sergeants, the Inspectors all collaborated to produce this evidence. Of course this is precisely what they'd bloody done.' Chesshyre quotes a DCI who told him 'the attitude of most people he knew socially was: "If you know he's done it, bloody well get him convicted." '

But police tactics during interrogation are not limited to crude violence and threats, nor to the fabrication of interview notes and verbal admissions. Many officers have an awareness of the psychological dynamics of interrogation and how these can be exploited. Chesshyre describes a police interrogation training session in which officers are encouraged to try to build up a rapport with the suspect. 'Try to make it seem as if you've got a common aim, and are moving towards the same goal. There's nothing wrong with being friendly.' This can go further. In the interviewing team 'one police officer . . . should cater for all a suspect's needs – food, drink, exercise, phone calls – so that the prisoner becomes reliant on that officer, building a relationship that might in due course lead to the suspect confiding in the officer.' *Police Interrogation*, a handbook for investigators published by *Police Review*, advises detectives on 'getting the customer into the Yes mode' and on the importance of 'isolation' in 'assisting the interview'. It requires no great feat of imagination to understand what impact such a combination of friendliness and threat could have had on someone as vulnerable as Paddy Armstrong in 1974.

In this context, the defence argument that you remember the abnormal and forget the norm loses some of its force. With the help of Sir Robert Mark, Paul Condon, and the officers cited by Graef and Chesshyre, it is not difficult to think of another answer to the rhetorical question posed by Lawson on behalf of the three detectives: 'Why fabricate the truth?' Even if things are different now, as Condon claims (and as Mark, a generation earlier, also claimed), there is no disputing that it has, in the recent past, been common practice for police to manipulate the rules and enhance their evidence.

This all stems from the well-documented tendency among the police to assume that the right man has been arrested – a tendency no less pronounced in 1974. In the same way that to a certain section of Middle Eastern security services any British businessman is probably a spy, to a section of the British police, when IRA bombs go off and an Irishman is arrested, two and three have been conclusively demonstrated to add up to four. The presumption of innocence, the right to silence, the right to legal representation, freedom from oppression and intimidation during questioning – the much trumpeted glories of our system of criminal justice – can too easily be reduced to nothing. Official suspicions about the Irish have powerful cultural and historical roots, as Roger Swift and Sheridan Gilley have pointed out in their book *The Irish in the Victorian City*. The Irish were Britain's first mass immigrants. Following the Great Famine, these impoverished refugees from a devastated rural economy arrived in Britain's newly industrialized cities and quickly acquired a reputation for violence, crime and dissolution:

The flooding of ghetto areas by impoverished and disease-ridden Irish, and the violence and social misery which was a by-product of such a brutalizing environment, together with a ready acceptance of the notion that Irish peasant society was inherently violent, formed for sizeable sections of the British public an explanation for all Irish troubles and misfortunes which rested on 'the fundamental weaknesses of the Irish national character'. A stereotype of the brutalized 'Paddy' was formed, in greater detail and enjoying wider currency than ever before: intemperate, improvident, violent, totally innocent of any notions of hygiene, mendacious and undependable – not so much a lovable rogue as a menacing savage. The popular imagination had, in general, little time for reflection on the environmental factors which dictated the over-representation of the immigrant Irish on the poor-law and crime lists, and in the alcoholic gutters. Weakness of national character was an easily accepted explanation. During the middle decades of the nineteenth century these prejudices were systemized with a somewhat crude anthropological typology ... Despite being white and, for the most part, English-speaking, the sense of identity of the Irish immigrant, his consciousness of himself and of his history, was sufficiently acute to present considerable difficulties in the way of early or successful integration.

No one living in Britain today needs the work of social historians and sociologists – valuable though it is – to understand that there exists an ingrained suspicion of the Irish.

I encounter frequent and (usually) good-natured jokes about my accent. On arriving at the offices of the *Guardian* recently I was asked to fill in a pass – something required of all visitors. Then the security guard joked: 'You need one, all right, especially with that accent.' It was not intended maliciously and I did not, I do not, take offence. But once Armstrong and the others were in custody, it is unthinkable that the officers who were about to interrogate them felt neutral about their suspects.

*

If there is a tendency in certain quarters to suspect that any Irishman accused of an IRA bombing is guilty, there is equally a tendency – usually found in the same quarters – to believe that policemen accused of being bent for the job are innocent. On the second day of the trial, in an unusual move, Mr Justice Macpherson permitted the defence to make an opening statement to the jury. This is a recent procedural development which has so far been restricted to complicated fraud trials, the argument being that it is unfair to the defendants in a lengthy trial for the jury to hear only the prosecution case at the outset. Macpherson's latitude enabled Lawson to counter Bevan's arguments immediately after they had been put. The benefits to the defence are obvious. But that isn't the issue. Apart from being extremely rare and confined to complex fraud cases, such opening statements by the defence are normally permitted only if the defence intends to call evidence. The rules are clear. In this case, the defence called no one. Macpherson's ruling therefore took on even greater significance. As indeed does his decision to permit the reading aloud to the jury of the signed statements made by Attwell, Donaldson and Style in the summer of 1990 in which they denied the charges and put forward such explanations as they could muster to support their argument that the rough typed notes were innocent. Such documents, unsupported by testimony, are known in law as 'self-serving statements'. A statement in which the defendant asserts his innocence and which is unsupported by testimony is a self-serving statement and as such usually ruled inadmissible.

As the trial progressed, the judge indicated what he thought of the case. On day eight – at the conclusion of the prosecution case – he suggested to the jury, as they were adjourning for lunch, that they might have heard enough. 'It may be, members of the jury, that you have already come to a view about this case. I have come to a view, at least about certain aspects of the case. Armstrong is not here, for example.' He told the

jury that if they wanted to dismiss the case against the detectives, they should send him a note after lunch. 'I will be here
at five past two,' he said. In the event, the jury did send him a
note, though not the one he had asked for. Their note was to
say they wanted to hear more and, in particular, they wanted
to know whether the police would be going into the witness-
box.

In his summing-up Macpherson told the jury that he would
be spending most of his time going over the defence case. That
was only right, he said, because it would reflect the relative
amount of time prosecuting and defence counsel had spoken
for. The defence case was far longer, he would be concentrating
on it. It is an approach rarely seen in normal criminal trials at
the Old Bailey, and one that seemed to puzzle Bevan; he was
to tell one journalist that it was the first summing-up he had
heard in which the judge had neglected to mention the prosecution case. He went over the defence arguments with great
thoroughness. Why had the detectives not destroyed the rough
typed notes if they had been sinister? They had had ample
opportunity. Where were the 'trigger notes' used to make up
the typed notes, if the Crown case was true? Macpherson
underlined the defence argument that the Crown case was at
best 'speculative', and quoted the defence assertion that a
'conviction would be a miscarriage of justice, an assault on
justice'. The three men before the jury were, the judge said,
'men of impeccable character, and that must weigh with you.'
Their failure to give evidence on their own behalf, and equally
their failure to call any evidence in support of their case, was
not to be held against them. It was 'negative evidence': 'the
defendants have to prove nothing, the Crown has to prove
beyond reasonable doubt that the manuscript notes were fabricated.' He told the jury it was all a very long time ago, and it
would be unfair to expect the defendants to remember anything of the detail. The jury was not to hold the officers' lack
of recollection against them. He suggested that the jury may

have been impressed with the evidence of Robert Huntley, a former commander of the Bomb Squad. In court Huntley had described Armstrong as 'the lowest of the low ... IRA cannon-fodder', the kind of expendable asset typically used for bombings such as that at Guildford. Huntley, along with Imbert, had also given evidence about Armstrong's interviews: neither had witnessed anything untoward and both were men of exemplary character and record. The judge reminded the jury of Armstrong's failure to report his mistreatment to the police doctor, and commented on Armstrong's non-appearance in court: 'it does seem significant to me.' He repeated the point put by Glass and Evans: why should the officers have put their careers on the line by fabricating evidence when they already had the truth?

When the jury retired to deliberate – a time when most defendants, even those on bail, are taken into custody – Lawson asked that unconditional bail be continued. 'Oh, yes, certainly,' the judge said. 'But please don't go far.' (In 1978, I was a remand prisoner as a result of a visit from Special Branch and saw from the window of my cell the forlorn figure of Jeremy Thorpe being trooped into Brixton Prison.) As a model for the treatment of suspects in criminal trials, Macpherson's behaviour cannot be faulted.

During the defence's closing speeches the jurors were told that they were the first to have 'the full picture'. Yet for a 'full picture' it was oddly incomplete. The jury did not hear Conlon's suppressed alibi evidence; they did not hear about the duplicate detention records; they did not hear about Carole Richardson's alleged Pethidine injection; or about Armstrong's emotional and psychological state at the time of his interrogation.

More than this, the jury heard nothing of the four men who could have told them most about the Guildford and Woolwich bombings – Brendan Dowd, Joe O'Connell, Harry Duggan and Edward Butler. Dowd and O'Connell, along with another man and two women (who have never been named because they are still at large), bombed the Seven Stars and Horse and Groom in Guildford; Dowd, O'Connell, Butler and Duggan took part in the Woolwich bombing. These men are in custody in English prisons, they confessed to the attacks in 1975, and in 1977 the Court of Appeal accepted the bulk of their admissions as true. They have never stood trial for Guildford and Woolwich, they have never even been charged. Yet the evidence that they were responsible is overwhelming.

Dowd came to England in 1974 to set up an IRA active service unit (ASU) in London. He, O'Connell and their accomplices lived lives of complete clandestinity, staying in rented flats under false names, using forged passports and driving licences, keeping away from the Irish community. IRA couriers kept them supplied from Ireland with arms, explosives and money. After setting up the London ASU, Dowd went to Manchester to establish another IRA cell there. He was arrested in Manchester towards the end of 1975. O'Connell took over the leadership of the London ASU, now comprising Duggan, Butler and a man named Hugh Doherty (Doherty did not join the ASU until after Guildford and Woolwich). They continued their activities until the siege at Balcombe Street in December 1975 – after which O'Connell, Butler, Duggan and Doherty were arrested. By this time the London ASU had killed nineteen people in over fifty shootings and bombings.

There is no doubt that between them Dowd, O'Connell, Butler and Duggan were responsible for Guildford and Woolwich. After their capture and certain that they would be going away for a long time, O'Connell and Butler made statements, first to the police, later to Alastair Logan, explaining how the attacks had been planned and executed. It was their evidence on which lawyers for the Four sought leave to appeal against conviction. In the 1977 hearing O'Connell, in the witness-box, was able to describe in detail the interiors of the Horse and Groom and the Seven Stars, how the bombs were made, who planted them, who kept lookout, who drove the cars. His account fitted in every way with eyewitness descriptions and forensic evidence. O'Connell said, for example, that Smith's watches, with four-and-a-half-volt batteries with screw terminals, had been used as timers on both Guildford bombs - all of which accorded with the forensic evidence.

Still more tellingly, he and the others were able to give evidence about aspects of the two attacks which the police had not revealed. O'Connell, for example, said he had worn a bush hat during the attack on the King's Arms, Woolwich -- a hat which he left behind in the stolen car. At the time, the car's owner had reported the theft to the police, but since it had not been connected to the bombing it had not been thoroughly checked on recovery. Once the car's importance was appreciated, it was traced. The owner confirmed that a hat of the type described by O'Connell had been found. O'Connell also said that, while he was planting the bomb in the Seven Stars, a soldier asked him about bus times. The police had a statement from a soldier who had asked about the last bus to leave Guildford. Dowd too offered something new: in an early interview with Logan he had made passing reference to 'two old men with shopping bags waiting for a bus' among the customers at the Horse and Groom on the night of the bombing (a detail not made known during the investigations or during the 1975 trial). In fact, two old men had been interviewed by the police shortly after the explosion. Their statements had never been disclosed to the defence. How could Dowd have known this if he had not been there? Havers, who was opposing the appeal for the Crown, was forced to concede that the statements had 'a ring of truth about them'; he went on to accept that 'a great deal of what [Dowd] says is true.' Havers was also prepared to admit that Butler was present at Woolwich and that Duggan was 'convincing'. The appeal judges, too, had to accept the force of the new evidence. Mr Justice Roskill said: 'We are content to assume that O'Connell's story of his presence [at Guildford] and participation may be true and that Dowd may also have taken part ... It is difficult to believe that had he [O'Connell] not been present on both occasions his knowledge of the detail ... could have been wholly invented.' What these details added up to was a coherent, logical story – in sharp contrast with the ramblings of Armstrong, Hill, Conlon and Richardson.

Supporting the oral testimony of Dowd, O'Connell, Duggan and Butler was scientific evidence linking the bombs at Woolwich and Guildford – in their construction, components and method of delivery – to a long series of bombings committed by Dowd and the London ASU from the summer of 1974 until their capture. The forensic evidence prepared by government scientists was withheld from the defence at the time of the trial. Sir John May has lambasted a different but in some instances overlapping group of government scientists for their conduct in the Maguire case. And they were criticized in scathing terms by the Court of Appeal last June in connection with evidence similarly withheld in the case of Judith Ward. Sharp-eyed jurors in the trial of the three detectives might have noticed a report which appeared in the *Independent* during the early stages of the prosecution case. The report said:

Two former government scientists criticized last year by the Court of Appeal over the wrongful conviction of Judith Ward will not face criminal charges. After a nine-month investigation by West Yorkshire Police, the Crown Prosecution Service said there was 'insufficient evidence' to charge Douglas Higgs and George Berryman, his assistant at the Royal Armament Research and Development Establishment. Last June, both men and a colleague, the late Walter Elliot, were castigated by the appeal judges ... They said the scientists 'concealed ... matters which might have changed the course of the trial'. Two years earlier, Mr Higgs and

> Mr Elliot had been criticized by Sir John May ... for hiding
> evidence from the trial of the Maguire family. They served between
> four and fourteen years for terrorism before being freed.

There was no mention in the trial of Attwell, Donaldson and
Style of either the suppressed scientific evidence gathered by
these discredited scientists or of O'Connell and the London
ASU. One would not have expected the defence to have
raised these matters, but surely it would have been in the
interests of the prosecution to do so. And Bevan had every
opportunity, none better than when Sir Peter Imbert came to
give evidence. It must be remembered that although Imbert,
like Commander Robert Huntley and Philip Havers, appeared
for the prosecution, he was called as a favour to the defence.
Imbert was the officer who negotiated the surrender at Balcombe Street after the ASU were cornered. It was Imbert,
together with his boss, Jim Nevill, head of the Bomb Squad at
the time, who interrogated Butler after his arrest. When questioned about his first operation in England, Butler replied:
'My first job, someone you've already put away for it.' 'Which
one?' 'Woolwich.' Nevill then asked: 'You mean the bomb
thrown into the pub, the King's Arms?' Butler replied: 'That's
correct.' Both Butler and O'Connell, in December 1975, told
Imbert and Nevill at some length of their involvement in
Guildford and Woolwich. They also said that the people
convicted for the bombings had not committed them.

Imbert is the man widely praised for bringing glasnost to
the Met. It would have been nice to hear him explain why it
was that, although he heard Butler and O'Connell confess to
the Guildford and Woolwich bombings, he said nothing to
bring it to light at the time or in Court Eight, apart from
mentioning it to the DPP. Imbert had, after all, been present
when Nevill said to O'Connell: 'Look, if it wasn't your team
then I want no mucking about. If it was, the matter must be
reported. We must do something about it.' But they didn't.

The police have often tried to suggest that the Guildford Four could have taken part in the attacks along with Dowd and the Balcombe Street men. But there is absolutely no supporting evidence for this theory. Analysis of the available forensic evidence – fingerprints, fibres and so on – gathered from the safe houses used by Dowd and the others has failed to turn up anything connected to Hill, Conlon, Armstrong or Richardson.

The trial in Court Eight lasted eighteen days. The jury went out on Tuesday 18 May at 10.15 a.m. They were unable to come to a decision and were sent to spend the night in a hotel. The judge continued the defendants' unconditional bail and the court rose. At 10 a.m. the following morning, after he had again spoken of the three defendants' exemplary character, the judge told the jury he would accept a majority verdict. The jury went out and returned at noon, when the forewoman delivered not guilty verdicts against each of the defendants. The judge discharged Attwell, Donaldson and Style, and, in a clear reference to the May inquiry, told the court that after this verdict he hoped it would be realized there was nothing more to be gained 'from gazing at the entrails' of this case. The reactions were predictable. Alastair Logan gave a bravura performance at a press conference, criticizing the way the prosecution had been handled and rehearsing, for the benefit of the press, the evidence of his client's innocence. Paddy Armstrong said he felt 'very bitter': 'The whole thing seemed to be about me and not the police officers. I feel I have been retried.' 'I realize that the detectives were just scapegoats,' Paul Hill said. 'But now nobody, not one person, has been made accountable for the things that happened to us. We were the only ones to suffer and we were innocent.' 'Our names have been slurred all over again,' Gerry Conlon said. An entirely different set of reactions came from Blackpool, where two thousand delegates had gathered for the Police Federation's annual conference. They received news of the acquittals with a standing ovation. Kenneth Clarke, who that day had addressed the conference, echoed the judge when he said he hoped 'a line could now be drawn under these old cases'. 'I think it was very wrong that the police officers were ever accused,' Lord Denning said. 'I have always had complete confidence in the police testimony in the Guildford case.'

The following day most leader-writers – in full hue and cry, demanding resignations and wholesale reforms when the Guildford Four were released – opted for retrenchment. The *Daily Telegraph* summed up the revised position:

> Until now the received view of the Guildford Four, at least since they were released by the Court of Appeal in 1989, is that they were all innocent victims of a scandalous miscarriage of justice who spent many years in prison for crimes they did not commit. The acquittal of the three ex-policemen, and some of the new evidence heard in the course of their Old Bailey trial, suggests there are reasonable grounds for suspecting that two of the Guildford Four, Mr Patrick Armstrong and Mr Gerry Conlon, might have been guilty after all. This raises the disturbing possibility that the real miscarriage of justice in their case occurred when they walked free.

The reference here to 'new evidence' is puzzling. The *Guardian* published Conlon's post-conviction confession three years ago; both it and Armstrong's similar confessions (the content of which was not revealed in Court Eight) were hardly 'new' – they have been available to the DPP since 1975.

While the jury was out I overheard a reporter explaining the situation to a TV cameraman.

'They were guilty, the Guildford Four, of course they were,' the reporter said.

'Really? I thought they were framed.'

'Nah. The cops just fiddled the paperwork a bit.'

'Like expenses?'

'Look what they did when they got out. First thing they did, they went and addressed an IRA rally.'

'Yeah?'

I stepped up and asked: 'Where was this?'

'Over in Ireland somewhere. It might have been Belfast. And they admitted to a whole string of atrocities, other murders.'

'You're kidding?' the cameraman said, clearly startled.

'IRA murders.'

'Which ones?' I asked the reporter.

'I don't know exactly which ones, but it's all coming out now in court.'

At the press conference given by Alastair Logan and Paddy Armstrong, a journalist, listening to Logan's analysis of the trial and the allegations against his client, turned to me and whispered: 'This is bollocks, isn't it?'

Personal prejudice is one thing. Allowing yourself and your paper to be manipulated is another, far graver matter. Yet this is precisely what has been happening. Crime and home affairs correspondents have told me privately that they have been the recipients of off-the-record briefings from senior police officers and cabinet ministers. No one will go on the record about these briefings, and it is frustrating to know about them and not be able to name names. Those who, since 1989, have been whispering that the Guildford Four are guilty will doubtless continue to do so, their confidence boosted by the verdicts in the trial of the three detectives. But they are not yet confident enough to repeat out loud what they say in private.

After the verdicts, I saw the defence barristers leaving the Old Bailey to head back to the Temple. I ran over and asked Anthony Evans why he thought the jury had acquitted. He was in expansive mood. 'Well, this was the first jury to have the full picture put before them.' 'How can you say that?' I asked: 'The jury didn't hear about Conlon's alibi, about the suppressed scientific evidence, about the Balcombe Street men.

'Why didn't you put that before the jury?' Evans turned away. 'Mr Evans?' 'No comment.' I then asked Anthony Glass if he would care to repeat what he had said in court about Armstrong being the bomb carrier. Glass told me he had no comment to make either. 'Why not?' I asked. 'Don't you understand English?' Glass replied.

During the trial there was another hearing going on at the Old Bailey. It concerned three police officers who have been charged with framing the Birmingham Six, and it was heard in camera. The full trial is expected to take place in late autumn. There has been an interesting development in the case. The man chosen to prosecute the officers is none other than Graham Boal. Boal it was who represented the Crown in the hearing when the Six were freed in March 1991. He had been instructed not to oppose the appeal but, while he conceded the men had to be released because of the glaring deficiencies in the evidence, nevertheless suggested that the Six were guilty. He therefore asked the judges, *pace* Rozenberg, to make a distinction between 'unsafe' and 'unsatisfactory' when delivering their judgment. This the judges rejected − such a distinction did not exist, they said, and no court had ever been asked to make it when overturning convictions. The judges also told Boal, who spent some time defending the original police investigation, that his address was beginning to sound like 'a damage limitation exercise'. Boal, the man who so recently stuck up for the Birmingham detectives, will now exert his best efforts to have them put in gaol.

A year after returning from Latin America, I was one of a large throng at a party to celebrate a publishing house's fortieth anniversary. Agents, authors and publishers mingled and exchanged news and gossip. It was a pleasant affair, the kind people in publishing know all too well. But I, having only just qualified for admission by the recent publication of *Stolen*

Years, was new to it and did not feel greatly at ease, though I noticed that Paul Hill, my co-author, seemed to be taking it in his stride. My uneasiness was intensified by the approach of one of the publisher's newly signed-up authors.

'Hello, Paul,' the author said affably.

'What about you,' Hill replied, unfazed by the newcomer.

'My spies tell me you've been at the Labour Party conference in Blackpool,' the author said.

'Gotta stay true to my working-class roots, know what I mean, Nigel?'

Nigel Lawson chuckled heartily and moved on.

The moment seemed surreal. It was an exchange I never thought I'd live to witness, as improbable as any of the possibilities I'd contemplated in Cuenca after reading of the Guildford Four's release. I joked about it to Hill in the taxi we shared after the party. He had enjoyed his banter with Lawson, so had I. But later I began to see the exchange in another light. I don't know what Nigel Lawson thinks about the Guildford case – I don't know *if* he thinks about it; certainly I can't remember him having pronounced on it in public – but somewhere in his jovial greetings it seemed to me there was something like 'No hard feelings, eh?'

'No hard feelings' may seem – in view of what Paul Hill, Gerry Conlon, Carole Richardson and Patrick Armstrong have been through – grossly, insensitively inadequate. But they have received nothing better, and have had to put up with a lot worse, so it is probably the nearest they will ever get to an official apology for the sixty years they spent in prison.

BIBLIOGRAPHY

Truth: The First Casualty by Michael O'Connell, Riverstone, 1993.

Proved Innocent by Gerry Conlon, Hamish Hamilton, 1990; Penguin, 1991.

Stolen Years: Before and After Guildford by Paul Hill with Ronan Bennett, Doubleday, 1990; Corgi, 1991.

Time Bomb: Irish Bombers, English Justice and the Guildford Four by Grant McKee and Ros Franey, Bloomsbury, 1988.

Trial and Error: The Maguires, the Guildford Pub Bombings and British Justice by Robert Kee, Hamish Hamilton, 1986.

Error of Judgment: The Truth about the Birmingham Bombings by Chris Mullin, Chatto, 1986.

The Fall of Scotland Yard by Barry Cox, John Shirley and Martin Short, Penguin, 1977.

The Politics of the Police by Robert Reiner, second edition, Harvester Wheatsheaf, 1992.

In the Office of Constable by Sir Robert Mark, Collins, 1978.

The Force by Robert Chesshyre, Pan, 1990.

Talking Blues by Roger Graef, Collins Harvill, 1989.

The Irish in the Victorian City, edited by Roger Swift and Sheridan Gilley, Croom Helm, 1985.

Death plus Ten Years by Roger Cooper, HarperCollins, 1993.